AMERICAN BAAPU

India Through My Eyes

By Rick Cormier

Other books by Rick Cormier:

◆ MiXED NUTS or What I've Learned Practicing
  Psychotherapy

◆ My Life Cracks Me Up

◆ Freestyle Community Drum Circles

◆ God Should Have Worked On Sunday... A More
  Likely Version of the Old Testament According To
  Rick Cormier

BAAPU

also "bapu." *báa-pu*

Hindi, from the Sanskrit word '*papu*' meaning "protector"

1. An affectionate term for father

2. Sometimes used in reference to Mahatma Gandhi.

Not Applicable: At 5' 11" and 220 pounds (180cm and 100kg), no one will ever mistake me for Mahatma Gandhi. ;-)

TABLE OF CONTENTS

FOREWORD

Normally, for a Foreword, an author finds an expert willing to validate him. The expert then writes several pages about how wonderful the author is and why readers should take him seriously. My "unofficially-adopted" daughter, Namrata Bhutani, had another idea. She suggested that I ask some of the young people of the Indian subcontinent just why they think of me as "Baapu", "Touji", "Angel Paa", "Baba", "Bade Papa", or "Dad".

So, it humbles me to present the Foreword of this book, written by some of the sons and daughters of my heart:

It was the month of June, 2016. I was reading my Quora news feed and stumbled upon a mesmerizing answer to a question where an American Quoran stated how he helped a young Bengali woman which led to his first trip to India! Moved by the answer, I messaged the Quoran who turned out to be a fellow musician! We became friends on Facebook. Since then, we conversed almost every day. Our bond developed. The virtual world was our home where we could talk our hearts out. I still remember how, on the night of 18th July, 2016, I was worried about my results for an exam. When I told Rick about this, he calmly said, "Don't worry, you'll always have my blessings." In India, we believe in blessings. "Blessings can do miracles," the Vedas say. "Here's my report card, Rick. I made it through!"

This was the first day I realized that Rick is not just a friend. He's a father figure to me. My 'Touji'. Rick calls me his "non-biological son". It was then he called me "Beta" ('son' in Hindi) for the first time. I can't explain the tremendous joy I felt. All I knew was that the bond we share is an immortal one. He's always been a true mentor.

Touji has a keen interest in India and its culture. He has profound knowledge about India in so many aspects. Sometimes I feel that he was born in the wrong country. Touji's "Dil hai Hindustani". (Touji's heart is that of an Indian).

Whenever I feel low, I talk to Touji. When I used to study for 12-16 hours a day, completely exhausted, and drained of motivation, Touji would give me the boost I needed. And that's what a father does!

When Touji decided to celebrate Diwali with us, I was on cloud nine. Finally, I'd be seeing him for the first time. Hug him tightly, never to leave.

There's a saying in Sanskrit, "Vasudheva Kutumbakam" ("The world is a global village"). For the first time I could feel the emotion of those two words. It's almost been a year knowing Touji, and there isn't a day I don't think of him. Our eternal love towards each other is the reason for the existence of this bond.

He is the epitome of optimism. There is never a day he said something that had even the tiniest patch of negativity. Touji's humor is impecca-ble.

"Your mental state defines your age." To me, Touji is an eighteen year old boy who lives his heart out. He lives each day like it was a year. He enjoys each moment to its fullest.

I kept the best part for the last: his love of music. In Hinduism, we be-lieve that the one who is good at music is blessed by the goddess, Saraswati. Touji is immensely blessed by Saraswati. Touji's videos are a delight to watch. He is so involved in music that his facial expression defines it all. Whenever those drums sing, the listener's feet have no other option except to dance. I'm eagerly waiting for those jam sessions that I'm going to enjoy with Touji when he visits me.

My life has changed since I met Touji. For all those little bursts of joy he has given me, for all those smiles he has left on my face after we talked, for all those little pep-talks he has given me, for all the immense love, for all the blessings that I count on, I thank Touji for all of it.

Nishchay Maheshwari
India

I found Rick on a website many years ago where he wrote something very lovingly about India. As soon as I started talking with him, I felt so much love for him! Soon I started calling him "Angel Paa", as he became the light in my life, always there to enlighten my path, to love me, to guide me, to help me. He is a guardian angel who is with me to this day! Rick has a very pure heart that sees the goodness in people.

Deepika Verma
India

It all started with an article on Quora. Who knew reading that answer on Quora would change my life? I reached out to Rick and said "thank you" simply for writing such a nice article and sharing his experience with the world. He replied back and the rest is history.

I'll share a very strange thing that my father told me. He is very spiritual and was told by several Indian astrologers that, when I move to United

States, I'll have help in the form of a second father, a guardian. Who knew that something so abstract would come true?

Rick often reminds me, "I am never far away". I know I am far away from my home. To visit my parents, I have to take a 20-hour flight to India. To see my American parents however, the flight is only three hours. I spent Thanksgiving with Rick and Judy in 2016. In 2017, I spent my Spring Break with them.

Rick is the happiest person I know. I have learned a lot of life lessons from him. I am grateful for all of his advice; I know it is from the best of his knowledge, experience, and heart. Rick taught me how to be happy, follow my passions, and live life. I feel more alive now than ever.

Piyush Arora
India/ USA

~:~:~:~:~:~:~:~:~:~:~:~

Unhappy, in a severely abusive marriage, I found myself searching for answers or validation that what I was thinking and feeling was normal. That is when I came across Rick's article about abusive relationships on Quora. One night, I messaged him. I didn't know if he would actually reply back, but he did. Looking back in hindsight, I am not sure if I would be able to go through the divorce process if Rick didn't walk me through my thought process.

Divorce was not easy. I was scared to step on the other side of fear. No one understood the trauma I was going through, the inner struggle for years, thinking to myself and lying to myself that one day everything will be okay. Rick helped me see the fantasy world I was living in and how it was affecting me and my children.

He was not only my guardian angel that time, but for many times after that. I am sure that he will always be. His words stuck with me: "Always do what you're afraid to do." I have lived by these words and have not been let down.

I got *myself* back, and Rick helped. I spent hours debating, arguing, asking him questions. He would patiently answer each one of them and not only would he answer, he would also share stories from his experiences in life.

The things I have been able to achieve in the last four years post-divorce are things I couldn't have achieved in my ten years of marriage. I am sure that, if I was still married, I would have never achieved what I have in life now.

Starting from scratch and accomplishing all that I have, as well as the confidence I resonate, is because of the support Rick gave me in his friendship.

Javeria Masood
Pakistan/ USA

~:~:~:~:~:~:~:~:~:~:~:~

Like an angel from God, Baapu came into my life when I was at my lowest point. Like a father, he listened to me, understood my situation, and guided me out of hell. He was happy when I was happy, sad when I was sad. It didn't matter how busy he was, he always had time for me and my issues. No amount of thank yous can ever express my gratitude for him. No words can fully express how I feel when he calls me "betiya".

Namrata Butani

India

~:~:~:~:~:~:~:~:~:~:~:~

I still remember the day when we started our conversation on 30th June, 2016, randomly on Quora.com. Yes, Quora should be given credit for our Indian-American family bond. I have always been a very reserved and shy person who rarely interacts with strangers, especially on social networking sites. This time, the case was different, because it was Rick on the other side: an intellectual, wise, kind, funny, sporty, loving, fatherly . . . overall complete package of enthusiasm and a "Young Ageless Soul in an Old Body". How could I have not enjoyed Rick's company? No chance.

Nandita Sudha Tiwari

India

~:~:~:~:~:~:~:~:~:~:~:~

Even though I am from Bangladesh, I grew up watching Bollywood movies. You know, where people start dancing out of nowhere and they are super popular and liked by everyone? Well, I didn't expect to be dancing all the time, but I imagined that, in America, I would make a lot of friends. However, that changed within a few days of arriving in America. People in Texas weren't that friendly, especially to those who don't speak English very well. I spent most of my time on social media instead of interacting with people. I felt depressed, and I withdrew.

I don't recall exactly what the question was, but I read an answer on Quora written by this wonderful American man who was very appreciative of south Asian culture. He shared a story about meeting an Indian girl in an airport and how they became friends. I loved the story. I was moved by how wonderful he and his wife were to an Indian girl alone abroad. How well they took care of her, probably knowing how out of place and scared she must have been. Though I didn't know anybody in this story, it somehow felt close to my heart. I came to follow this wonderful man on Quora. Later, I read his post about how he actually went to India to be in her wedding and his experience of India. It was a beautiful story.

Rick has this wonderfully enthusiastic personality. Every time I talk with him, I feel so energized. And he really listens. It's funny that we never met, and I really didn't think he would even reply to my message, but he did, and he didn't make me feel like just another one of his Quora followers.

I remember telling him recently that I tasted a new food at lunch and how I enjoyed it so much. Later, I discovered that it wasn't permitted in my Islamic religion. I am not a very religious person, but it still didn't feel right. The next day I got a message from Rick who said he did a bit of research and found that it was a man-made rule, not originating from the Quran but centuries afterward. It was perfectly okay for me to indulge on something I liked. And that is Rick, taking the time out of his day to think about and help someone.

When I told him how awkward and shy I felt and how I didn't have any friends, he suggested I smile and say hi to a few strangers each day. And I did! And it felt good! Now people smile at me sometimes.

I don't think I can describe the energy that I feel after speaking with Rick, but he has an evergreen personality and every time I see his big smile I think, "That's who I want to be".

Saila Islam
Bangladesh/ USA

~:~:~:~:~:~:~:~:~:~:~:~:~

I came across this awesome gentleman, Rick, whom I now call Dad, through Quora. I was surfing Quora once, and I stumbled upon an answer related to travel in India. Reading that answer gave me goosebumps. Never had any answer on Quora impacted me the way his answer did. His answer displayed the fascination he has for Indians and the Indian culture. He observed and loved every minute detail about being in India and had poured his heart out in that answer.

I couldn't resist but send a personal message to him saying that he had described India better than any Indian could have! I am so glad I did that. For that one message led to an amazing journey of an Indian girl becoming a "daughter of the heart" of an American man!

He replied in a humble, polite way, as always, after which we connected on Facebook. We got to know each other and, with every passing day, we grew closer. Soon I realized that he genuinely cared about my problems. I started turning to him for any problems I faced. His positive, motivating words kept me going. He shared my pain and comforted me when I was low. He was always willing to lend a helping hand whenever I was in need. He is now my pillar of encouragement who constantly motivates me. We have talked about a ton of things. Be it family, friends, politics, movies, arranged marriages, Sindhi culture, partition of India, his next trip to India, his books, his bands, his love story, his life lessons . . . the list is endless. We are never short of topics to talk about.

He also patiently listens to all the details of the India-Pakistan partition stories and how it affected us Sindhis, as well as the stories of my meetings with prospective grooms! Occasionally, I would answer his questions on Indian culture that he could not ask other Indian friends. He went from being my inspiration, my mentor, my therapist, my motivator, my grammar teacher, and my friend — to being my Dad. How I wish I would have met him earlier in my life!

He taught me to be grateful for every little thing life has given me. He taught me that being happy is a *choice*. He restored my self-esteem and turned me into a bundle of positive energy. I am happier than ever all because of my young, energetic, rockstar Dad!

Look for a happy drummer with the sweetest smile on the earth. That's how you'll spot him! He has an amazing sense of humour. The epitome of optimism, he is a source of positive energy. He is always up for help-ing others. He gets a sense of purpose when rescuing someone.

Quora changed my life. It showed me that a stranger on the other side of the world with a different nationality, skin color, race, caste, lan-guage, culture, and religion can become family. Now that I am ready to settle down in life, all that I look for in my potential partner is a glimpse of my American Dad.

Neha Photani
India

Opening Reflection

My dad was a bigot.

If you didn't share his heritage, culture, race, religion, or nationality you were, somehow, less than him. This had no influence on me because he seldom talked with me or my brother, and I didn't even realize he was a bigot until I was eighteen. By then it was too late.

I was already influenced by my mom. I often say that my mother was "color blind". She could distinguish colors just fine but she loved people. She didn't see *race*. Whether I brought home friends who were black, Chinese, or Puerto Rican, my mother's only question was, "Is he going to stay for supper?" or "Does he know I'm making a Japanese dish tonight?"

My mother never sat me down and said, "Treat everyone the same". She just *lived* it. It was who she was. She loved *everybody* unless they gave her a reason not to. When my mom made a Polish friend, she learned to speak Polish. When she began making Jewish friends, she learned Yiddish. She saw other cultures as undiscovered oceans to swim in.

I am my mother's son.

I say that with pride. My mother died at age 92, long before we moved from the Northeastern US to the Southwest. She would have loved Santa Fe, New Mexico. She would have loved to meet our American Indian friends who live in the Pueblos here. Given a month, she would be speaking Tewa and Keresan. My mother would have loved the connections I made in India. She would be learning Hindi phrases, using them, and then telling me what they meant. She would have written me a letter in Hindi — with a translation on the back.

She was an incredible cook who made dishes from all over the world. At age 16, she won an original recipe contest. You could point to any spice in her considerable collection of spices and she could list every use for it. While my father and my older brother scoffed at her ethnic fare, preferring more typical American cuisine, I loved trying foods from all over the world.

My mom would have mastered Indian cooking.

She was also the warm and affectionate one in the family. If my mother knew that there were a bunch of young people in India who had become like sons and daughters to me, she would be delighted. She would want to know everything about every one of them. She would talk about them as though they were her own. They would even start receiving greeting cards from her and birthday gifts she couldn't afford.

I think that I was always the piece of my mother that reached beyond herself. While her parents forced her to drop out of school at age thirteen to clean houses, I got a post-graduate degree. As an adult, she was a voracious reader. Though she was not allowed to finish high school, she wrote articles in our local newspaper all her life. She got me started writing when I was thirteen-years-old. She said, "Write about what you care about." After she was married, she worked in factories. Neither she nor my father drove a car. She traveled only once in her entire life. She left an incompatible marriage after twenty-two years and never remarried.

My mom was smart, creative, affectionate, and she loved people. When you got her talking, she could go on forever.

During the last conversation we had before she died, she looked so thin and frail in her hospital bed. She held my hands and told me how proud she was of me — as a son, a husband, a father, a psychotherapist, a writer, a musician — proud of the person that I had become.

With tears in my eyes, I told her, "All of the *best* of me, I got from *you*." We don't always get to say that to the people who deserve to hear it.

My mom would have loved the title of this book and my relationship with each of the young people mentioned in it. She would have loved the idea of my family expanding to include their families and theirs expanding to include mine.

I dedicate this book to my late mother, Dorothy Cecile Cormier, because the best of me I got from her. None of this story would have happened without her influence.

Everything and everyone we encounter is a mirror. Positive people see the positive and negative people see the negative because we are all looking for external proof of our own internal experience.

We bring to the table precisely who we are.

The story that follows is true. The relationships and the experiences are all real. This is not something I could have intentionally made happen. I wouldn't begin to know how. My wife, Judy, and I share a philosophy: everything will either be a great experience or (eventually) a funny story. I show up with an open heart and with as few expectations as possible. I help others when I can. If that has resulted in the life I'm living now — well, lucky me!

~:~:~:~:~:~:~:~:~:~:~:~

To see the people and places mentioned in this book, go to www.rickcormier.com/american-baapu-photos and see photos marked by page numbers.

Why India?

I was around twelve-years-old when I first read about a country called "India". It was a country where people practiced spirituality/religion in their daily lives, not just for an hour on Sunday mornings. I read that, though 81% of Indians were Hindu and only about 13% were Muslim, most Hindus didn't eat pork out of respect for their Muslim neighbors. This intrigued me. I tried to imagine American Christians refraining from eating pork and shellfish out of respect for American Jews.

Yeah, right.

People said that Hindus worshiped cows, but I learned that wasn't quite true. Hindus view cows as the most peaceful and giving creatures on earth. They see cows as the ultimate mother figure. As such, Hindus hold a deep *respect* for cows. They don't worship or pray to them as you might a god. All of this led to my early fascination with India, and it got me in trouble at school.

I was born Roman Catholic and sent to a Catholic school for my early education. At the age of thirteen, I listened to my teacher, a Catholic nun, talk about how everyone in the world who didn't "accept Jesus Christ" was doomed to hell.

I took religion very seriously at that age. I raised my hand and said, "So, the monk who owns nothing and spends his life meditating high in the mountains, believing that he is in direct contact with his idea of God, is going to hell, and all I have to do is dress nice on Sunday and sit through a mass in Latin and I get to Heaven and he *doesn't?* That doesn't sound very fair to me."

The nun didn't know how to respond, so I was sent to see *the priest,* which was much worse than being sent to the principal's office. Only those who were in dire trouble were sent to "the priest". After I explained my budding view of world religion, the priest said, "I wish more young people your age thought this hard about these matters. I, personally, have faith and wish you luck on your spiritual journey. Don't stop asking these difficult questions."

He didn't send me to hell. But, over the next few years, I decided that I could not remain Roman Catholic, or even Christian, if it meant believing that I was *better* than other people around the world. If there was a "God," he had to think more *globally* than the Roman Catholics did.

It's one of our human failings: my country is better than yours. My race is better than yours. My religion, my sexual orientation, my culture, my school, my profession, my neighborhood, my car, my kid, my team . . . all better than yours. As American Christians we were taught that our "club" was the only one eligible for eternal reward. Let's be honest: I was only Catholic because my parents were. They were Catholic because *their* parents were. Generations of Cormiers have been Catholic because all Acadians were traditionally Catholic. It came with the culture. How could I worship a being who favored one culture over all others? It didn't sound very godlike.

I learned that Hindus and Buddhists don't think this way at all. They believe that the sort of person you are counts for something and that any spiritual path has value. I learned much later that Christians in India are as tolerant of other religions as their Hindu counterparts. Throughout my teens, I considered myself an agnostic until I discovered the Unitarian Universalist Church where Christians, Jews, Buddhists, Wiccans, Atheists, and others share the same pew.

When I was in my twenties in undergraduate college, I contracted to do a two-year, twelve-credit multimedia program on Mahatma Gandhi. As part of my research for that project, I interviewed Morarji Desai, the Prime Minister of India, at the United Nations Plaza Hotel in 1978[*].

Thanks to an Indian friend in Houston, Texas, I make a great cup of homemade masala chai (chai tea), spiced with cardamom, cloves, cinnamon, black pepper, and fresh ginger. I love Indian food. I love drumming for kirtans. I love Bollywood movies. The 2006 American film, "Outsourced," which takes place in India, is probably my favorite movie of all time because, unlike "Slumdog Millionaire", it portrays India and Indians realistically and respectfully — and because it's a great intercultural love story.

My heritage is Acadian, but India has been a part of me for most of my life.

~:~:~:~:~:~:~:~:~:~:~:~

---

[*]Anyone who is interested can read the article I wrote about that interview on my website: www.rickcormier.com

In May of 2014, while heading home from our son's college graduation in Ohio, we were stranded overnight with 15,000 other airline passengers at the Dallas, Texas airport due to the cancellation of all flights. This happens a lot in Dallas. American Airlines said we *might* get a flight to Albuquerque, New Mexico the following evening.

While in line for Customer Service, I noticed a young woman in line behind me who looked anxious. I struck up a conversation with Nipanjana Patra, a young astronomer from the city of Kolkata* in West Bengal, India, who was visiting the U.S. for the first time. Like Judy and me, she needed to get to Albuquerque and was told she couldn't get a flight until the following evening. We took her under our wing and made her part of our small entourage. American Airlines had promised that they would issue cots, blankets, and pillows to those travelers who had to sleep in the airport overnight. They failed to mention that there would only be one cot per twenty or thirty travelers. We kept Nipanjana safe and even found her a rare cot on which to sleep.

The next morning, Judy cleverly observed how people were managing to get morning flights out of Dallas. She arranged for Nipanjana to get an earlier flight, secured an additional seat on the same flight, and insisted that I accompany Nipanjana to ensure her safe arrival in Albuquerque. Judy followed on a flight shortly afterward. During the flight, Nipanjana took out her laptop computer and showed me photos of the radio-telescope she designed and built in India as part of her PhD work.

---

* Formerly known as Calcutta. In the years following India's independence from England, 25 Indian cities changed their names. Madras became Chennai, Bombay became Mumbai, etc.

Waiting in New Mexico for Nipanjana was Miller Goss, the former head of the "Very Large Array" (VLA) in Socorro, New Mexico. It is an astronomical radio observatory that consists of 27 radio antennas, each 82-feet (25m) in diameter. The data from these antennas is combined electronically to give the resolution of an antenna 22 miles (36km) across. The 1997 film "Contact" with Jodie Foster took place at the VLA. Miller would be hosting Nipanjana at the VLA as well as providing for her accommodations. Miller Goss is a radio astronomer credited for having discovered a part of the Milky Way. I knew none of this when I told him, "Take good care of her. She's pretty special." When I said goodbye to Nipanjana, I hugged her and said, "My family just grew by one."

To thank us for taking care of Nipanjana, Miller invited us to take a professional tour of the VLA later that week. It was an up-close tour reserved for professional astronomers and grad students. After the tour, he took us all out to dinner and then to his home.

I happened to mention on Facebook that we had been out with Nipanjana and Miller at his home in Socorro, New Mexico. One of my Facebook friends is an amateur astronomer. She wrote me, "You met *Miller Goss*? You had beers with *Miller Goss*? Do you have any idea who he *is*?" When I told Miller about her comments, he shrugged it off. He said, "I'm not so special. You tell her that I have nothing but admiration for amateur astronomers. You wouldn't believe how many important discoveries have been made by amateurs."

Before Nipanjana left New Mexico, she and Miller drove to our home in Santa Fe. Nipanjana admitted that she was tired of eating

New Mexican food, so we went out to our favorite Indian restaurant. Though the restaurant is Punjabi[*], they were happy to cook her the Bengali dishes she requested. Afterward we returned to our house where we played music for the two of them and Nipanjana sang a classical Indian song for us.

She, my wife, and I became friends via email and Facebook. She referred to us as her "American parents". Once, when a friend took a picture of us wearing western hats at the Santa Fe Rodeo, she posted that picture on Facebook and called us her "cowboy parents". When she announced her marital engagement in the winter of 2014, she asked that her American parents attend her wedding in Kolkata, India in March of 2015, not just as guests, but as a part of her wedding party.

Which is how, at the age of 62, I finally got to visit India.

---

[*]Punjab and West Bengal are two of India's 29 states. What was once known as East Bengal is now the country we know as Bangladesh.

Part One
TRIP TO INDIA: 2015

WELCOME TO KOLKATA

We expected Nipanjana to send relatives to meet us at the Kolkata Airport, but she came to welcome us herself. It was an emotional greeting with lots of heartfelt hugs.

Once we all got into a taxi, my initial impression of India was of its frenzied traffic. It was NUTS! We were shocked by the congested, loud traffic. I was prepared to see vehicles driving on the left. WRONG. Driving on the left is only "suggested". Drivers drive wherever there is an opening, including the middle and the right side of the road! We saw no marked lanes in the cities. Vehicles come within an inch of other vehicles and pedestrians, and no one seems even mildly surprised. After a few days of this, you come to realize that these drivers are much more skilled than us Westerners at navigating this sort of traffic. Vehicles blow their horns constantly, not because they are angry but to let others know that they are there! A blaring horn usually means, "I'm here", "I'm about to pass you", or "I'm approaching a corner".

What's more, Kolkata's traffic includes cars, trucks, buses, push carts, three-wheeled auto-rickshaws, bicycle rickshaws, motorcycles, motor scooters, bicycles, and pedestrians — with an occasional farm animal joining in the fun.

But here's the thing: as crazy as this traffic is, everyone is calm. Close-calls are ignored. When a vehicle flies past a pedestrian close enough to brush their clothing, there is no negative reaction whatsoever. There is an innate trust shared by vehicles and pedestrians.

How to drive in major Indian cities: blow your horn as you position yourself alongside any vehicle in front of you. Blow your horn again and cut them off as quickly as possible so that you are now in front of them. While doing this, bear in mind that every vehicle behind you is attempting to do the same to you. You do this even when traffic is practically at a standstill. After a few days of this, one learns to relax in Indian traffic. You learn to trust your driver and the drivers around you.

At one point, Judy reacted to a near-accident by exclaiming, "Holy Cow!" Then she added, "I probably shouldn't say that in India, huh?"

We arrived in India on the day they celebrate a festival called Holi, the spring festival of colors, sometimes known as the festival of love. It's a very joyous festival of people tossing colorful powders at one another as well as colored liquids. It is often portrayed in Bollywood movies for the strikingly beautiful visual appeal and gaiety. I later learned that drinking "bhang," a potent cannabis-based smoothie, is also popular among some Indians during Holi.

Nipanjana warned us that we might not wish to go outdoors that day because of Holi. Judy and I had different thoughts. If we were going to be in India on Holi, we were going to join in the fun! I brought my best white shirt just for the occasion.

Because of the time zone difference, we had left New Mexico, USA on Wednesday and landed in India on Friday. As tired as we were from the flight, we donned our white shirts and left the apartment. A woman outside the front door wished us "Happy Holi!", and we wished her the same. She asked, "Are you going to join in?" We said, "That's why we are wearing white." She said, "Then let me be the first to put colors on you!" She proceeded to smear each of our faces with bright yellow powder.

Next, we joined a group of celebrators nearby. Adults smeared our faces, hair, and clothing with greens, blues, and reds while children sprayed us with colored waters from super-soakers, pails, and buckets. Adults often offered us their colors so that we could do the same to them.

Next, we decided to take a walk down the crowded street. Initially, we would get apprehensive looks from people — probably wondering if we had been showered in colors against our will. As soon as we smiled and wished people "Happy Holi!", their faces and smiles beamed. More adults smeared us with colors. One man looked at us and said, "You don't have any *pink*! You need some pink!" and proceeded to rectify the situation.

Many of these adults spoke Bengali, the native language of West Bengal, but no English. It didn't matter. We communicated just fine. We came upon groups of kids and teens whose hands were black, caked with colors. They lined up to shake our hands, all of us laughing the whole time. Two men we met had heavy coatings of colored powders on the front of their shirts and trousers. Each approached me and gave me a huge, tight hug! More laughter. One guy said, "On the day of Holi, we're *all* the same color."

What a first day in India! What an introduction to the people of India! We met them at their best, and they met us at our best. It reminded me of my community drum circles, where people with nothing apparent in common gather together and PLAY. Whatever differences between us — culture, politics, religion, race, income, profession, sexual preference, nationality, and language — are irrelevant when we play together. That's what Holi was for me. I was a person from another culture celebrating joy itself — celebrating being alive — with the people of India.

Nipanjana's family arranged for us to stay in a "service apartment" in the city of Kolkata in West Bengal, India. West Bengal is a coastal state to the east of central India. A service apartment is a long or short term furnished apartment with many of the amenities of a hotel, including room service.

Also attending Nipanjana's wedding were other "international parents" including Miller and Libby Goss of Socorro, New Mexico, and Ron and Jay Ekers of Sidney, Australia. Miller and Ron were both former Directors of New Mexico's Very Large Array. We shared an apartment with Miller and Libby while Ron and Jay had one a few floors up.

The manager of the Kolkata service apartment was a short, chunky, eager-to-please guy in his 40s named Aditya. He was great. We told him what we wanted for breakfast the next morning, and he made it happen. We asked for a pot of masala chai, and it appeared within the half hour. But Indians don't drink as much coffee as we do, so morning coffee was about half a pot for four people, enough for a tiny cup each. We eventually asked for two pots each morning.

Bathroom showers are interesting in that the shower head is mounted on the wall, rendering the entire bathroom a shower, with a drain on the tile floor near the toilet. When showering, most things in the room get wet or damp, including the toilet seat, the towels, and the toilet paper (when there is some). The floor tiles remain wet for hours afterward.

We were fortunate that our apartment had Western-style toilets and toilet paper. That's not always how it's done in India. Most Indians, especially in northern India, squat over an opening in the floor, clean themselves with their left hand, and have a water source handy to clean up afterward.

This practice may sound strange to Westerners, but I've heard some very good arguments in favor of it. For instance, imagine you are hot and sweaty from rigorous work or exercise and need a shower. Instead, someone hands you a box of tissues and suggests you simply wipe yourself clean. Or imagine yourself holding an infant who poops all over your hand. Would you wipe your hand with tissues and consider it clean?

This may be too much information for some readers, but it's a significant cultural difference. It's why you learn not to eat nor hand food to others with your left hand (which, as you might imagine would seem disgusting to an Indian).

Although most Indians eat food with their right hand and use no utensils, our apartment came equipped with spoons. We made a habit of boiling tap water to kill any bacteria and using it to wash our plates, cups, and spoons. Before coming to India, I had done some research. I learned that Westerners should avoid India's tap water since it contains bacteria we don't have the antibodies to combat, that can very likely lead to dysentery. Experienced travelers recommend that you use only bottled water, even to brush your teeth! It was during our stay in this apartment that we learned these new habits.

Speaking of cultural differences, a few of the more humorous differences that became apparent in my first few days were:

1. Lots of people pick their noses here. Not privately, when no one's looking, but publicly! A beautiful woman on the street might look you right in the eye while her finger disappears up her nose digging away! Picking one's nose in public isn't the social faux pas that it is in Western culture.

2. Some men pee in public. In the two and a half weeks we were there, I'd estimate I saw this seven or eight times. Now and then you'll see a guy stand on the sidewalk furthest from the street, faced away from traffic, having himself a whizz. I'm told that this is due to the scarcity of public facilities.

Some days we went out for lunch. In the evening, Nipanjana's family cooked food for us and had a family member deliver it, a 45-minute drive. The food was consistently wonderful. Bengalis don't use the heavy, spicy sauces we Americans associate with Indian cuisine. Bengalis believe in letting the flavor of the food come through, so they spice their food primarily with turmeric, as opposed to the more complex curry mixtures. They also cook with more fish than we might associate with Indian cuisine. Nipanjana once told me that in her parents' home, at least one meal per day was fish.

One afternoon, Nipanjana's brother, Goutam, brought us to Millennium Park in Kolkata, a beautiful 2.5km private park, where I saw hundreds of black and gray house crows for the first time. We took a ride down the Ganges River on a large tour boat and saw the best sunset of our visit. It looked like a gigantic glowing orange ball disappearing behind the cityscape.

In the mornings after breakfast during our week in Kolkata, everyone would sit around reading or checking email or doing work on their laptop computers. I checked email and read Facebook messages quickly, because I was itching to get outdoors. I was in India!

I began taking morning walks by myself and came upon a fairly poverty-stricken area of the city. I always felt safe. My smiles were usually returned, and I learned to say two things in Bengali: Hello and Thank You, Namoshkar and Dhanyobad. I struck up conversations with some individuals who spoke English. We talked about politics, religion, culture, and life in general. I also made friends with some people who didn't speak English.

One such soul was a thin, disabled guy whose right arm was scrunched up by his side. He sat on a wall watching his two young daughters play. They were around six or seven years old and played with a small scooter and a broken bicycle. I was pretty tired after having walked for hours, so sitting on that wall looked appealing. I put my hands together in greeting and said "Namoshkar", and he returned the gesture. While we both watched his daughters play, the little girls smiled shyly at me from time to time. When his daughters did something cute, silly, or troublesome, the man and I would look at one another and only communicate through nonverbal looks or gestures. When I left to head back to my apartment, we gestured goodbye. Every morning after that, I saw the father and his daughters at the same place, and each time we waved hello. That may not sound like a deep friendship, but it was an important one to me.

A similar meeting happened a day or two later. During my walk, a boy of ten or eleven with a pleasant manner began walking by my side. He didn't ask for money; we just traded occasional smiles as we walked. Sometimes I would take a picture and then show it to him. This always made him smile. At one point, I asked him his name. He looked at me and said nothing. I thought that he probably didn't understand the question.

After we walked for several more blocks, he pointed to me and asked, "Name?" I replied, "Rick". He then pointed to himself and said, "Amit". Amit and I walked a few more blocks until another boy approached him, saying something in Bengali. Amit waved goodbye and ran off.

Talking about religion and politics comes straight from the head. It involves passing life through an intellectual and rational filter. But non-verbal communication comes straight from the heart. It requires being present and just putting yourself out there. Even now, that father and Amit are stronger memories for me than any of the people I spoke with during those walks.

Judy wasn't very comfortable when we walked the streets. There were often no sidewalks in our neighborhood so you had to walk on the edge of the traffic. The constant blaring of horns and vehicles rushing inches beside us made her understandably nervous. I was comfortable with it from the start.

I was reminded of the Huichol shaman whose culture taught that the souls of the dead went like liquids into a big pot while waiting to be reborn. He said that, sometimes, the soul of one culture gets mixed into the soul of another. When that person is reborn, he or she will always be drawn to that foreign culture. I told Judy that my Acadian soul must have gotten mixed up with one from India.

My unofficially-adopted son, Nishchay, has taught me to say, "Dil hai Hindustani" ("I have the heart of an Indian.")

One afternoon, Judy and I visited Kolkata's Birla Temple. It's a beautiful building inside and out, where cameras and shoes are not allowed beyond the entrance gate. (Fortunately, there are plenty of pictures of it available online.) Judy and I took turns seeing the temple. One of us stayed with the shoes and cameras while the other went into the temple.

The temple consists of five or six individual shrines, each with its own alabaster statue of a Hindu god, some decorated with flowers, and each manned by a priest. The priests usually wear orange, yellow, or white robes or long kurtas in these colors or any combination of the colors. I watched as devotees prayed at each shrine before approaching the priest who blessed them and handed them something I couldn't see. At one point, a priest spotted me standing at a distance and gestured for me to approach. He gave me a solemn blessing and handed me six tiny sugar confections.

After Judy had returned from her temple visit, we prepared to leave. One of the temple guards approached us and gestured for us to stand on the temple steps while he took our picture with my camera. "What a nice guy!" we thought. He took three photos. When I thanked him in Bengali, he insisted I owed him 100 rupees!

Child beggars, whose feet have never known shoes, are more likely to coax rupees from my pocket than temple guards in uniform who behave as though I had agreed to pay for a service. I told him that I didn't have 100 rupees, and we left.

Nipanjana had come to our apartment with one of her mother's saris for Judy to try on to see if she would like to wear a sari at the wedding. She looked great! Judy decided that she would like to wear a sari, so we all went shopping at FabIndia, Nipanjana's favorite clothing store. Judy chose a beautiful deep blue and gold sari. I bought three kurtas. The store didn't carry the underskirt needed for the sari, and they didn't make or sell blouses to match, so the next day we went to New Market to shop for those.

New Market was built in 1874 by the British, whose disdain for Indians made shopping at Indian bazaars repulsive to them. The market area was originally housed inside the Victorian gothic building, and access was limited to the British. Today, its 2000 plus vendor stalls are located outside as well as inside that building, offering a wide variety of items including apparel, electronics, jewelry, handicrafts, and foods. The indoor vendor stalls look like small shops you might find at any local mall. The outside stalls look like typical Indian bazaar stalls. The market is so extensive, there are guides who, for a small and negotiable price, will help you find the vendor or items that you need.

New Market is not for people who dislike crowds. You might be shoulder-to-shoulder with people shopping. You just insert yourself into a crowd that is moving in the general direction you want to go, and let them inch you along to your destination. We got everything we came for, but moving through the crowds was a challenge best taken with a healthy sense of humor.

Nipanjana's Wedding

Indian weddings are famous. They can last three to five days and are very lavish. Bengali weddings are even more so.

The day before the wedding there was a pre-wedding party for the friends and family of the bride which we called the "bachelorette party". It took place at Nipanjana's parents' home. Nipanjana had asked for Judy to bring a flute to play. She knew it wasn't practical for me to bring a drum to India, and I had assured her that I could make a plastic bucket or a cardboard box sound musical.

After Judy played a flute solo, I was handed a plastic bucket to drum on while accompanying Judy on another flute piece. After that, I was asked to play my first ever "bucket solo". It was a big hit (pun intended).

Two of Nipanjana's relatives came to our apartment the following day to help Judy with her sari. There is a real skill and art to wearing one. I had ordered a hand-stitched Bengali sherwani in advance. A sherwani is an ankle-length, fancy, formal men's tunic. Mine was light blue trimmed with pearl white and decorated with hand-stitched silver embroidery. Anyone who knows me recognizes that this is a bit fancier than my usual jeans and button-down shirts. Before I ordered my sherwani, I sent a picture to Nipanjana and asked whether it was appropriate or too fancy. She assured me that it was perfect for a Bengali wedding. When we arrived at the venue, I noticed that all of the men were wearing slacks and button-down shirts! I said to Judy, "These guys are all dressed like Americans! Am I the only guy dressed Bengali?" Later, it became clear that the fathers and brothers of the bride and groom also wear sherwanis. Whew! The wedding was quite lavish and detailed and is where we met the groom, Raunaq, and his family for the first time.

There are many various rituals that take place in the days before the wedding, but on the day of the wedding a special turmeric ceremony takes place in which the bride, at her home in the company of friends and family, is covered in a turmeric paste, creating a yellowish cast to her skin. Sometimes the groom, at his home and with his family, participates in this ritual also. The color yellow is considered auspicious. The turmeric paste is believed to ward off evil spirits while purifying the body and mind before the wedding ceremony.

The bride and guests arrive at the wedding before the groom. The bride wears an elegant sari, red being a popular color choice, and lots of jewelry, often in gold. The groom arrives later, no longer on horseback or atop an elephant, but generally by car. He is dressed in white with an elaborate headdress called a topor which to western eyes looks like the top of a fancy wedding cake.

In the wedding ceremony, the groom sits waiting for the bride. Then the bride enters holding large leaves in front of her face and sits beside the groom. She lowers the leaves and their eyes meet. Nipanjana's sister blew into a conch shell many times, which is an integral part of a Bengali wedding. Next, the groom places the sindoor (vermillion paste) on the spot where his bride's hair is parted. This signifies the change in her marital status. The couple each place large, long garlands over one another and walk in a circle around a fire seven times. After this beautiful ceremony, the guests bestow their blessings, followed by a delicious feast.

At both the pre-wedding party and at the wedding itself, we ate traditionally with only our right hand. This was a first for us, and we got through it just fine. The food was amazing. I tasted curried jackfruit for the first time. I thought it was some sort of high--quality meat. Delicious! Not only did I have seconds (possibly thirds), I now make it myself at home.

The day after the wedding ceremony, a formal reception is hosted by the groom's family. In this case, the groom's family lived in Tamil Nadu, a state in southern India. At this point, Judy and I parted ways from the festivities and flew to Jaipur for the second part of our trip.

WELCOME TO JAIPUR

As I mentioned earlier, visiting India has always been my dream. I had long ago decided that if I could visit only one city in India, my first choice would be Jaipur, in the desert state of Rajasthan. Located on the northwest side of India, Rajasthan, "Land of kings", is India's largest state. Jaipur, nicknamed "The Pink City", was founded in 1727 by Maharaja ("high king") Jai Singh II and is known for its historic palaces and forts as well as its rugs, clothing, and jewelry. Some credit Jaipur with being the first "planned city," as the streets, sections, and gates were designed in advance.

A two-hour flight brought us from Kolkata to Jaipur. Air India had upgraded our flight, which was the first time I've flown in first class. I hadn't had leg room on a plane since the 1970s! An online Quora friend in India wrote, "Now as you have enjoyed the Bengali traditions, be ready to get the Royal treatment in the Land of Kings in Jaipur". Well, the "Land of Kings" indeed! Our hotel room at Jas Vilas had a marble fountain built into the bedroom floor. We had breakfast by the pool each morning to the sound of birds and sitar music. We even had a party-sized bathroom.

The first morning, we took a walk around our new neighborhood. We didn't pass many people on the street, but we did see some incredible architecture in the local homes. We purchased drinks and snacks from local outdoor shops, and Judy found a shop where she purchased a beautiful long kurti (women's tunic) for 1100 rupees, about $17.00 USD, which included custom alterations by the shop owner. It was done and ready to be picked up about an hour later.

Though Jaipur traffic is not quite as chaotic and congested as Kolkata's (but still formidable by Western standards), Jaipur adds oxen, camels, and elephants to the traffic mix. Large animals in traffic became such a common sight, I wouldn't have been surprised to see a giraffe walk down the street carrying Jehovah's Witnesses tossing pamphlets.

In Jaipur, we mostly traveled around by private car. You could rent a car and driver for about 800 rupees ($13.00 USD) for four hours or 1400 rupees for eight hours. We had a few favorite drivers who made it a point to show us photographic opportunities and turned us on to the best places to shop and to eat.

It was also in Jaipur that we first tried riding in an auto-rickshaw. This is a three-wheeled vehicle that puts you right in the traffic. It's a much louder ride — you have to practically yell at the driver — but, because it's an open vehicle, you can take pictures unencumbered by glass windows. Auto-rickshaws, commonly called "tuk-tuks", are also much cheaper. We had one awesome auto-rickshaw driver for 10 hours at the cost of 500 rupees ($8.00 USD).

I read that "public displays of affection" are not acceptable in India, but I saw many young couples walking with an arm around one another. I can understand why hand-holding would not be popular in India. One person would get stuck holding the dirty hand. But Judy and I are big hand-holders. We do it without a thought. We held hands in India. No disrespect meant. This is who we are. We did refrain from making out in the back of an auto-rickshaw in the middle of traffic. ;-)

Jaipur had lots of attractions compared to Kolkata.

The Hawa Mahal is breathtaking. The 50-foot high Hawa Mahal looks like a palace but it is actually a facade constructed of red and pink sandstone and shaped like Krishna's crown. Royal ladies used to watch festivals and processions unseen behind its 953 windows, as they were not allowed to show their faces.. Most of its floors are only one room deep, built of different colored marble with inlaid panels, stained glass, or gilding, with ramps that access the upper levels where visitors can see a memorable cityscape.

Amber Fort was another of our favorite visits. It was the Maharaja's summer palace. It looks quite rustic from the outside but is most beautiful on the inside. With its many large ramparts, gates, and cobbled paths, the palace was constructed of red and yellow sandstone and white marble overlooking Maota Lake. The palace consists of four levels, each with its own courtyard. One of the most impressive features of the Amber Fort is the Hall of Mirrors, which served as the Maharaja's audience chamber. Imagine mosaic tiled walls where many of the tiles are mirrors. Supposedly, there are so many tiny mirrors in this section of the palace that it can be lit by a single candle.

We climbed up a steep mountain foot road on the outskirts of Jaipur and then down the other side to get to the Monkey Temple or "Galtaji". Built into a mountain pass in the Aravalli Hills, it is actually a series of temples that honor the Hindu monkey god, Hanuman. A natural spring exits high on the hill, supplying fresh water to a series of seven sacred *kunds* (water tanks) where thousands of pilgrims come to bathe each year.

We passed countless wild rhesus macaque monkeys along the paved footpath. Many British tourists described the area as filthy and smelly on TripAdvisor but that was not our experience (and Judy has a keen sense of smell). They also described the monkeys as "aggressive," often snatching food from their hands. When we arrived at the entrance to the footpath, several vendors tried to sell us snacks to feed the monkeys. We declined. As a result, the monkeys we passed simply watched us or continued sunning themselves or playing. If you sat and posed for a photo among an entire monkey family, none of them would bother you.

Jantar Mantar was one of five astronomical observatories built by King Jai Singh II who had a passion for astronomy. This one in Jaipur is the largest, and the best preserved and maintained. Built using astronomy and instrument design principles of ancient Hindu Sanskrit texts, it consists of 19 architectural structures which allows the observation of astronomical positions with the naked eye. The world's largest stone sundial is located at the Jantar Mantar and is accurate within two seconds.

At many of these tourist sites we were the only non-Indian tourists visiting. One of the interesting things we observed about Indians was that so many loved to have their pictures taken. We were often approached by Indians who asked us to take their picture. (Bear in mind that the picture would be taken with *our* camera and they would never see the result.) Sometimes they wanted us to pose with them, and sometimes they didn't. Sometimes one would have a cell phone camera to take the pictures but not very often. It was strange, but it let us meet and talk with some very nice adults, teens, and children.

When we were at Amber Fort, Judy was wearing a very stylish, wide-brimmed hat she bought in New Orleans. A teenage girl approached Judy and asked to take her picture. Then the girl shyly asked Judy if she could try on her hat. The girl began posing with Judy's hat as if she was posing for a Vogue magazine cover while her friend snapped pictures with her phone.

At Handicraft Haveli, Judy and I jammed on a huge drum and drew an appreciative audience. Even the staff was surprised to see two post-middle-aged foreigners rocking out on drums. Then Judy got to play a transverse flute. A salesman named "Lucky" asked me if I played guitar (Why would he assume that?) and handed me his. I played a few instrumentals for him while he recorded it on his smartphone. Before we left the store, he gave us a gift of a small statue of the favorite Hindu god, Ganesha, who symbolizes good fortune and the removal of obstacles. Today, that statue sits proudly among our modest collection of Indian souvenirs.

While in Jaipur, we contracted a driver to take us to the town of Abhaneri, 60 miles away, to see the Chand Baori and its nearby Harshat Mata Temple. The Chand Baori (deep well) is made up of 3500 steps descending 13 stories below ground. Constructed in 800 AD, it was used to collect precious rainwater and also as a community gathering place since the temperature at the bottom of the well was always five to six degrees cooler than at the top.

Next door to Chand Baori is the Marshat Mata Temple. It was built between the 7th and 8th centuries and subsequently destroyed by Islamic invaders during the 10th century. It remains an architectural and sculptural wonder, though some of its original columns and statues lie scattered about the temple courtyard. The priest of that beautiful little temple was among our favorites. He was friendly and hospitable and took pride in talking about his temple and the goddess Harshat Mata, the goddess of happiness and joy, to which the temple was dedicated.

Goats wandered free all over this temple. As we walked the long, wide stone staircase to and from the temple, we were joined by goats casually walking the same staircase. In fact, there were goats walking freely all over the town of Abhaneri.

A few more interesting observations about India:

1. I found one brand of beer: "Kingfisher". We found only one brand of wine, "Sula", but it comes in both flavors: red and white. An internet search says that there are more brands in India, but we never saw anything but Sula wine and King-fisher beer served. Feel like a soda/pop/tonic for the taste of home? There were both kinds: Coke and Pepsi.

   Alcoholic beverages are expensive in India. At one restaurant, the charge for a glass of wine was the same as the charge for both of our full dinners ($4.50 U.S.). When we settled the bill for our six day stay in Jaipur, the charge for *all* of our meals, bottles of water, afternoon masala chai, *and* washing our laundry was the same as the charge for five 350ml (half-sized) bottles of wine and two beers ($90. USD).

2. At restaurants, the *man* is handed a menu first. His order is taken first. His meal is put down in front of him first. He is asked how the food is. Make no mistake, the woman is treated like a queen, but it's clear who they consider king. For a westerner, it's an awkward cultural shift.

It was in Jaipur that we first shopped at an outdoor bazaar. What a blast! Both tourists and locals shop at these bazaars. Prices are pretty much set for tourists but, if you haggle, it becomes a game:

Shop-owner: "Sir, let me show you a nice wool scarf. Feel how in-incredibly soft this is. Only 4500 rupees ($72.00)."

Rick: "No thank you. I don't need a scarf."

S: "For you, Sir, 4200 rupees!"

R: "I don't need a scarf."

S: "Sir, how much would you be willing to pay for a scarf like this?"

R: "1000 rupees."

S: (laughing) "Sir, I couldn't sell a scarf like this for so little!"

R: (laughing) "That's okay. I don't need a scarf. I don't even wear scarves!"

S: "I tell you what, Sir, I will sell you this scarf for 4000 rupees."

R: "No, thank you."

S: "Sir, let's compromise. How much is this scarf worth to you?"

R: "1000 rupees."

After ten more minutes of this, I left with a woolen scarf for 1000 rupees ($16.00). My Indian friends tell me I probably could have had the scarf for 500 rupees, but fair is fair. It was worth what I was willing to pay.

I got a 2500 rupee calf-length cotton kurta (men's tunic) for 1000 rupees, a pair of 3800 rupee camel skin slippers for 1400 rupees ($22.00,) and, of course, a 1900 rupee drum for 650 rupees ($9.75). Indians expect to haggle. They make a game of it and have fun playing it. As long as you're willing to walk away, you can get some real bargains. I bought a good supply of Assam tea and some fresh cardamom for my homemade masala chai for a fraction of its cost in the United States.

The only really stupid purchase I made was the pair of camel skin slippers. The shop owner asked me how much I would pay, and I quoted a price considerably lower than he was asking. When he finally agreed to that price, I felt committed. After making sure the slippers were a good fit, I paid him. When I got home and looked at the camel-skin shoes or slippers with the curled-up toes and the dangling red yarn pom poms, I thought to myself, "When would I ever wear footwear as ridiculous as this? I wouldn't even wear these around the house! What was I thinking?"

One funny side to bazaar shopping is that every shop owner tries to get you to look at his goods. Some are aggressive about it, but most approach it with humor. If you sit and look at what he has to sell, a merchant might offer you some masala chai. A few shop owners even offered me a beer. On one occasion, I accepted a beer. They brought me a tall can of cold beer with a paper towel wrapped around the can to disguise its contents. When I finished the beer, I removed the paper towel. It was a Kingfisher beer, of course!

Judy got similar good deals by being willing to walk away from any purchase. In two hours time we didn't get further than one city block, but shopping at these bazaars was a lot of fun. Each stall is no more than ten feet wide. Imagine *miles* of outdoor shops like this!

Most Indians are vegetarian. In the cities, we found "non-veg" selections, mostly chicken, and sometimes mutton which, in India, may refer to the meat of sheep or goat. McDonald's "Big Mac" in India comes in chicken or paneer (cheese). At Domino's Pizza all pizzas are "personal pan" size, by US standards and chicken is the only non-veg topping. One doesn't find beef or pork in northern India.

One thing that Indians don't understand about Americans is our food choices. In India, one eats Indian food. One eats Italian food in Italy, Japanese food in Japan, Mexican food in Mexico, and so on.

The US is a mix of many cultures and nationalities. We don't eat "American food" (hamburgers, hot dogs, barbecue, macaroni and cheese, etc.) everyday. I might eat Polish food on Monday, Italian on Tuesday, Chinese on Wednesday, New Mexican on Thursday, Indian on Friday, Thai on Saturday, and broiled fish and a baked sweet potato on Sunday. I'll admit that I've been spoiled by so much variety.

Bearing that in mind, I was getting tired of eating Indian food every meal. I needed a change of pace. We ordered pizza at our hotel restaurant. It was a big mistake; they ordered it from Domino's. It arrived about an hour and a half later, was about 10 inches wide (the only size they make), and it had this white stuff on it they call "liquid cheese". It tasted nothing like cheese and was more like a thin white sauce. Fortunately it was only a 10 inch pizza.

During our trip to Abhaneri we stopped for lunch at a small town restaurant. In small towns and villages, most of the restaurants are vegetarian. I'm a dedicated omnivore, but I managed to find a delicious dish with noodles, mushrooms, and a spicy sauce.

It was hard to leave Jaipur and the Jas Vilas Hotel. We loved our room and breakfast by the pool and afternoon pots of masala chai. I'll always remember the guard at the gate who saluted me every morning. He never understood a single word I said, but we genuinely liked one another. Maybe it was because we both had the same huge grin, straight from the heart. Some things you just can't fake.

WELCOME TO DELHI

I made the following entry on my Facebook page, *"It is 12:50 AM. Judy is fast asleep. A driver will pick us up at 2 AM to bring us to the train station. Our "super-fast express train" leaves at 2:50 AM for Delhi. We expect to reach Delhi at around 8 AM."*

I woke Judy. We checked out of our hotel and headed to the train station by car. The train station was confusing and, unfortunately, the information desk was closed at that hour. One of the railway workers got us to our train car and helped us with our luggage. We now had three major bags. We had bought so many clothes that our two checked bags weren't enough, so we bought an extra bag before leaving Jaipur. As practical as this was, we were charged an additional $105. USD for the extra bag when we flew home.

Once in Delhi, we hired a car to take us to our hotel. Delhi traffic made Kolkata look like a small, peaceful village. We thought we were used to India's traffic, but Delhi held some surprises for us.

In Delhi, when traffic gets backed up, motor scooters and motor-cycles will drive *onto* the sidewalks and blast right through the pedestrians! We saw six motorcycles in a row do this. Pedestrians just calmly move out of their way and go about their business.

Our hotel in New Delhi was beautiful. The Hotel City Star was very modern, with glass, stainless steel, and marble, although our hotel room was smaller than our room in Jaipur. It is the first hotel I've ever seen that had art on the walls that I would actually own, nothing like the cheesy art we've come to expect in U.S. hotels and motels.

Anxious to see New Delhi, we decided to go out for a morning walk. The street was pretty crowded. A gentleman approached us and told us that it was dangerous to walk on this street:"too many dishonest people on alcohol or drugs who might rob you". We explained that we were just looking for an ATM nearby, but he insisted that we would be smarter to hire an auto rickshaw to bring us to one.

We wondered if he was scamming us. By the time we reached the next corner, a policeman approached us with the same warning! He waved down an auto rickshaw, negotiated the fare for us, and off we went. When we got back to our hotel, I asked a manager about the safety of walking on the street, and we got the same warning from him. "You don't take walks on crowded streets in Delhi. Tell the hotel staff where you need to go, and we'll hire you a car or an auto rickshaw. We'll negotiate the price, so that you're not overcharged, and take down the driver's information before you leave."

I was crushed. Exploring India on foot up to this point had been such an awesome experience. I had met so many nice people during my walks. Was Delhi, India with crime?? Was Delhi unsafe India? One cab driver explained to us that many people come to Delhi from other states looking for work. He said that because they are not from Delhi, they don't feel the same pride and ownership that people often feel toward their own home states and towns. As a result, some behave in Delhi in dishonest ways which they wouldn't do at home. In all likelihood, the people who warned us were originally from Delhi and wanted to keep us safe. We abandoned our walks and hired cars and auto rickshaws to get around. We had a great time in spite of this.

One afternoon, we visited the National Mahatma Gandhi Museum. I've been an admirer of Mahatma Gandhi for much of my life. For me, the visit to the museum brought back many memories from the two-year Independent Study project I did on him in undergraduate school. I remembered many of his quotes and speeches and read some for the first time. For much of his life, Gandhi fought against discrimination based on race, religion, and caste. Today's India, though much improved, still struggles with the issue of discrimination. People are still very much aware of castes, as well as Hinduism vs Islam. Today, even skin tone has become an excuse to discriminate. The museum visit triggered powerful emotions for me, especially surrounding Gandhi's assassination.

I noticed that, in the states outside of West Bengal, people greeted one another with "Namaste" instead of "Namoshkar". I had grown accustomed to using the Bengali greeting and continued to use it in Jaipur and Delhi. No one seemed to mind. I began teasing Judy by warning her that I was going to start greeting people by putting my hands together reverently and saying simply, "Dude".

Our auto rickshaw driver recommended a restaurant that serves Indian and Chinese food. I ordered a Chinese dish involving crispy noodles, chicken, vegetables, and sauce. When I told Judy that it was my favorite meal yet, she laughed at the fact that I had come all the way to India and my favorite meal was Chinese! Indian friends tell me that, in India, Chinese food is second in popularity after Indian food! I still love Indian food. I also love New Mexican, Thai, Cajun, Polish, Italian, German, Portuguese, and Acadian food, but you won't see me eating any one of those for each meal every day for weeks.

One thing I had found online in Delhi, that I knew Judy would love, is "Mystery Rooms." Participants are locked in a room for one hour with the missions being: 1) find the bomb in the room and 2) diffuse it. Judy loves solving puzzles and mysteries, so we made reservations. Once we were brought into the room and the door was closed, the lights immediately went very dim. "Hey! The lights went out!" shouted Judy. The professional and serious game operator, who probably chuckled as he watched players on his monitor, opened the door, grinned, and said, "That's part of the mystery. You have to figure that out!" and closed the door again. We both laughed.

We wasted about 10 to 15 minutes just getting the light back on. At one point, I flipped a switch we weren't supposed to touch and the room went completely dark. Even the television monitor went dead! The game operator had to come back into the room and straighten it out.

It was uphill from there. We found clues and figured them out. We found keys and opened locks. We solved puzzles. Just before we found the bomb, a voice recording came on announcing that we had 10 seconds before the bomb exploded . . . 9 . . . 8 . . . 7 . . .

Judy said, " If we're going to go, we'll go in each other's arms." We held one another, laughing.

"BOOM!" went the recording. Out came a puff of stinky smoke.

We were toast.

The game operator came back in and showed us the answers to the puzzles we hadn't yet solved. I suggested he stock T-shirts that said, "I DIED IN DELHI."

It was fun.

With only two days left before flying home, we considered traveling to see the Taj Mahal until we were quoted $150 USD by a very sleazy salesman to travel there by car. It seemed like a lot of money to spend an entire day seeing one building, so we passed. I later learned we could have gone there by train for about $10 USD.

I got a Facebook message from our friend Ashok Nalamalapu in Maine. He strongly suggested we visit the Akshardham Temple while we were in Delhi. I looked it up online. Akshardham Temple is the largest Hindu temple in the world. Sitting on 100 acres, it took five years, 300 million man-hours, 7000 sculptors, and 3000 volunteers to build it. There is no iron or steel framework, only pink sandstone and marble. It looked pretty impressive, so we called Satish, our favorite driver in Delhi, and arranged for auto rickshaw transportation for the day.

When we got to a spot on an overpass where you could see the Akshardham Temple, Satish stopped the vehicle and suggested I take a picture from that perspective. Satish parked his auto rickshaw and waited for us. (This is how it works when you hire a driver for a period of time. They wait around while you eat, shop, visit, whatever. Invite them to join you for lunch and they refuse.)

The first disappointing news was that photos are not allowed once inside the complex. The next disappointing news was that we had to check our cameras, cell phones, and *any* electronic devices. We got in line to check them and were told that only one of us could do that. So, Judy took my things and volunteered to go. Twenty minutes later we were in line for the security check.

Security? For a temple?

The women's line went smoothly and quickly. (Everyone knows that there are no female terrorists). The men's line hardly budged. I was behind literally hundreds of men, all Indians. If I had my cell phone on me, I would have called Judy and said, "Forget it!". Wherever she was, there was no way to contact her. Somewhere far ahead there were plastic trays, like at airports, to deposit your watch, keys, rings, belts, and any other metal objects. After nearly an hour, I finally passed through Security. As it turned out, I had a small extra camera battery in my pocket. I was told to go back to the place where we had checked our phones and cameras and surrender it there. Fortunately, I didn't have to go back to the end of the men's line.

After more than an hour in the security line, I was allowed to enter the grounds where Judy was waiting. She commented on how it is usually the women who have to suffer long lines. I pointed out that they checked men more thoroughly because they *could*, and that a security guard could stick his hand down a guy's pants, and the guy would think, "Well, this is awkward." But, try doing *that* with a woman! Once inside the grounds, the temple was worth the wait. For the best look at this amazing temple without the plane fare or the long lines, watch the YouTube video at https://youtu.be/69PIMDGv4Bg

I later discovered that in 2002, the Akshardham Temple in Gujarat had been the site of a terrorist attack that resulted in the deaths of 33 people and injury to 80 others. These security measures in Delhi were clearly implemented as a result.

When we first flew to India, we left on a Wednesday and arrived in Kolkata on Friday. Thanks to the mystery of time zone crossing, when we returned home, we left Delhi on Saturday morning and got home on Saturday night, despite the fact that it took about 34 hours to get there.

I wouldn't have traded one bit of this trip. My walks in Kolkata, the wedding, the Gandhi Museum, Akshardham Temple and everything about Jaipur was so memorable. We each bought lots of Indian clothing because it's so beautiful and comfortable. (Fortunately, any ethnic clothing is considered fashionable in Santa Fe.)

Make no mistake: there is garbage, there is poverty, there is pollution, there is corruption, there is chaos. One sixth of the world's population is crammed into an area about one third the size of the continental United States. But there is also a deep spirituality and humanity which directs daily life. There is economic and technological progress. India is one of the oldest civilizations on earth, and embodies a deep spirituality and humanity that directs daily life. The people are some of the warmest and most open-hearted that I have had the pleasure to meet. It is a culture that finds every excuse to celebrate joyfully. Stepping into India, one is bombarded everywhere with sounds, colors, and every form of art. India has a beauty that will stay in my heart as long as I live.

Part Two
WIDENING THE CIRCLE

I was so excited about our first trip to India in 2015 that I announced it on Facebook and Quora.com before we left. A few Indians on Quora asked me to write something about my experience when I got home. Two days after we returned, I wrote a slightly briefer version of the chapter you just read. It included photos. I called it my "India travelogue".

When I wrote it, I sincerely hoped that my humorous description of Indians picking their noses and peeing in public wouldn't offend anyone. Instead, the consistent comment I got from Indian readers was about my apparent my love of India. I wrote it hoping to please the two or three Indians who wanted to read about my experience of their country. What I didn't expect was that well over 100,000 Quorans in or from India would read it.

When you sign up to "follow" someone on Quora, it means you're interested in reading anything that person writes on any subject. Before writing that little travelogue, I had a few hundred Quora "followers," mostly because of questions I answered about psychotherapy and partly because I had once listed my favorite Bollywood movies.

Over the next few years, I gained more than 10,000 followers. The number grows daily, even as I write this. Many of those Quora followers sent me messages privately, expressing their appreciation of my assessment of India. Many suggested we visit *their* state or city if we should ever return. Some were ambitious and found and friended me on Facebook. In both cases, dialogues began. Online conversations covered many topics. When some of my online Indian friends in their twenties faced challenges in their lives, they would reach out and ask my advice. I often couldn't advise them by *American* standards. I had to fully understand *their* culture before I could be of any help. We got to know one another very well.

In The Meantime...

During this period, I was writing my last book, "MiXED NUTS or What I've Learned Practicing Psychotherapy", a memoir with psychotherapy insights and methods told in very plain language and with humor. When I completed the chapter on domestic abuse, I realized it was somewhat humorless, unlike the rest of the book. I wondered whether that chapter was a "fit". I uploaded an early draft of the chapter on abuse to Quora as a test to see what sort of reactions it would get.

The posting received very little *public* response, but I got private messages from more than three dozen women, mostly asking, "If my husband (or boyfriend) does *this*, would that be considered abuse?" I answered each of those private messages. In some cases, the women thanked me, and I never heard from them again. In other cases, I spent months supporting women through their personal processes of separation, divorce proceedings, career planning, and child custody battles. I mention this because several of those abuse victims were young Hindu and Muslim women who became part of my international family.

Becoming "Baapu"

Okay. So, I'm an American who fulfilled his lifelong dream of visiting India. I then wrote a nice article about the visit that lots of Indians enjoyed reading. I posted something I wrote about abuse and helped some abused women. That didn't make me anyone's dad, except my own son's, but sometimes life takes us in an unexpected direction.

A Hindu woman in her twenties wrote to me about how she walked away from her marriage after three months of verbal abuse. Her parents said, "Now, no man will want you." "You'll never have children." "You're the wife! It's your job to change him!" I chatted online with this young woman almost daily, offering her much-needed support. Her parents thought she was being over-dramatic, basing their opinion on her abusive husband's stable job and his charming public face. As a psychotherapist, I've worked with hundreds of abused women. I know that the abuser's charming public face is a lie. It's an act. I know that abusers systematically destroy their victim's self-esteem to make themselves feel clever and powerful in an unhealthy way. I did what I could to help.

This young woman did a brave thing. She walked away from her marriage after three months. That is rarely done in India. Traditional Indian society expects a woman in a bad marriage to suffer for life. When an abusive marriage does end, the abuser can walk away and find another victim, with no loss of respect. But by traditional standards, the abuse victim is often considered tainted. This was a tough thing to learn about India. As in so many countries and cultures, women often get a lousy deal.

Another young friend wrote me and said, "OMG! My parents have decided that it's time for me to have an arranged marriage! What should I do?"

This young woman was focused on her career. She had once been in love with a guy who loved her in return, but her parents disallowed their marriage because he was from a different state. Like many traditional Indian parents, they felt best qualified to choose a husband for their daughter. I have to admit, my mother couldn't even choose a *shirt* that I would want to wear. I couldn't advise this young woman about arranged marriages without first completely understanding the custom. I asked lots of questions and she answered them.

I learned that, today, many young Indian women have the right to say no to any prospect. They can decline to meet the prospect based only on his Facebook profile. If both are interested, then they meet in the company of their parents who ultimately decide whether this is a desirable match. Sometimes the help of an Indian astrologer is sought.

I suggested that, since the young woman wasn't meeting any guys at work, she could let her parents show her the online profiles of prospective suitors. She could refuse as many times as necessary and may even see a guy who actually interests her. Armed with her new non-committal attitude, she *did* look at guys online and she *did* say no. Until one particular prospect caught her attention.

She was excited to tell me about this guy who she really liked. After chatting online, they began texting and sharing phone calls. It was frustrating that he was in another country (and time zone) and was often unavailable. Finally, he announced that he would return to India in a few months to meet her. He later told her that he would be meeting *six* women during his visit, and would marry the one he liked best.

She was crushed. She had been focused on him exclusively, and now it turned out she was simply a contestant in a pageant where he was the Grand Prize. We talked about this extensively, and the result was she successfully rescued her dignity and self-esteem. This helped her avoid being as vulnerable again, particularly with online interactions. She cried. She gained strength. She recovered. She told him to take her off his list of prospective brides.

Most of the young Indian women I know want a romantic marriage. They want to be deeply in love with a guy who is deeply in love with them. The problem is most traditional parents don't teach their children anything *useful* about relationships. They don't warn daughters about abuse and control issues. They don't teach them to expect equal or loving relationships. As a result, many young Indian women get excited when a guy expresses interest in them — as if that were enough. When I ask, "How do *you* feel about *him*?" they are often thrown off guard because they are seldom asked *their* opinion. Young women will send me a photo of their latest suitor as though his looks are enough of a qualification.

One young woman has an emotionally abusive and controlling father. She doesn't only want to get out of her parent's home, she wants to leave India permanently and doesn't want to get married in order to do so. She hopes to pass a very difficult exam that might qualify her to apply for a job with the Indian Consulate or diplomatic services. When she gets discouraged, we talk.

I've helped young people cope with and prepare for the competition and pressures of higher education in a country where over-population influences so much of what westerners take for granted. I've helped fine-tune resumes and prepare young people for job interviews. In India the competition for good jobs is fierce. No one wants to wind up selling flowers in traffic.

One young friend wanted to be a psychologist. Her father disallowed it, because he didn't consider it a profitable or respectable enough profession. Instead, she took his advice and studied law. She excelled in college, survived all of the rigorous training and testing, and is now a full-fledged lawyer — with admittedly no passion for the job. I'm told that, in India, even in a field like psychology, it's not enough to have a Master's degree. Because of the competition, a doctoral degree may be required for even the *chance* at securing a desired position.

One young college student in India poured her heart out about her controlling boyfriend, things she had been ashamed of from her past, and her dreams for the future. She said that she couldn't talk with her parents about the things she talks about with me.

There is the thirty-year-old mother, living in the United States, whose ten-year marriage had been verbally, physically, and sexually abusive. Like all abusers, her husband convinced her that his actions were normal responses to *her* behaviors, and that everything he did was ultimately her fault. We spoke online each night for many months. I helped her realize and accept that it was her husband who had an incurable mental health problem, not her. In the end, she eventually recovered her self-esteem, left her husband, found an apartment, and got a job. Her children also began to thrive emotionally from the positive changes in their mother and their environment.

Today, that young mother is quite successful. She has won awards and been the subject of several magazine and newspaper articles. She has given talks addressing the subject of domestic abuse. She once told me that she wouldn't date anyone unless they talked to me first. I thought she was joking. Nearly a year later, when a lawyer wanted to date her, she insisted that he talk with me first.

These wonderful people, along with so many others, have become my international family — the "unofficially adopted" sons and daughters of my heart. When they come to me to vent, to ask advice, or to share their triumphs and disappointments, they get the same priority that I give my own son, Mike.

When I first mentioned in Quora and Facebook that Judy and I might return to India in 2017, the reactions were immediate: "You must stay with us!" The invitations ranged from Punjab, far in northern India, to Kerala at the southern tip. When looking at a map, I discovered that, "Come to Kerala!" was like saying, "You're coming to Maine? You must stop and visit me in

Florida!" The distances just weren't practical. Also, these young people were aged nineteen to twenty-nine. Would their parents welcome us into their homes? They didn't know me or my wife. When I raised this point, the responses were usually, "*My parents know exactly who you are. I talk about you all the time!*" "*I already mentioned this to my parents, and they're eager to welcome you and your wife.*"

It's one of the greatest honors of my life. The friendship, love, and caring that I share with these young people has resulted in my being called *Angel Paa, Baba, Touji, Bade Papa, Guardian Angel, Papa Rick, Dad,* and *Baapu*. I am forever grateful to have made such connections with young people I so admire.

With a timeframe of thirty-three days to plan for, I checked the map and chose five cities in the northern half of India — Delhi, Jaipur, Ujjain, Indore, and Amravati, which are the homes of some of the young people with whom I was closest and was eager to meet. I would have loved the opportunity to return to Kolkata to see Nipanjana's family again but, even by plane, it was two and a half hours from our nearest location.

Other dear friends we wouldn't be meeting during this trip included Archana, Saila, Akhil, Trupti, Ashish, Prachi, Suvarna, Shubhra, Jessica, Arun, Smruti, Darsika, Shubhi, Humay, Wasim, Subhodip, and Javeria.

There is one more thing I would like to say about "Becoming Baapu". These young people found me and friended me online. When they shared their personal concerns, I responded with love, respect, and as much wisdom as I could muster. Not as a psychotherapist, but simply as a person who might be able to help. Those without problems who extended a hand of friendship to the American who wrote so positively about India found in me someone who felt honored by their friendship.

When Judy was pregnant with Michael people would say to me, "I bet you're hoping for a boy." I used to tell them that I would love a son or a daughter equally. They are two completely different relationships, and I would enjoy either one. Then came Michael Richard Cormier, the best son I could ever imagine, and I love him dearly. He is smart, talented, handsome, and has a good, kind heart. He is an only child, and I secretly wished he had a sister so that Mike would have a sibling and because I'd be the father of a daughter.

Life can be funny. Sometimes, God or the Universe gives us exactly what we need, even if not in the form we expect or the timeframe we imagine. I'm in my 60s, and I suddenly and unexpectedly have daughters! I didn't catch them when they took their first steps. I didn't drive them to school or help them with homework. I didn't get to make them laugh by acting silly. They are from the other side of the world. They speak languages I don't understand. They grew up with religions and cultures that differ from mine. Their skin tone is even different from mine.

But make no mistake: This life has blessed me with daughters who I love dearly.

. . . and a few more sons.

. . . and I was about to meet some of them for the first time!

Part Three
RETURN TO INDIA: 2017

ENGLAND'S LAKE DISTRICT

Judy's dream has always been to visit the Lake District of England, so our trip began with a week there followed by two days in London.

I'll be honest. I've never had even the mildest curiosity about England, but, if India was *my* dream, England's Lake District was Judy's.

It was gorgeous! Between the quaint towns, peaceful lakes, soft mountains, lush trees, and old stone houses, my camera got quite a workout. We reserved a room at the Oakfold House Bed & Breakfast in Bowness-on-Windermere. Its owners, Max and Marnie, were outstanding. They were the sort of people we would hang out with if it didn't require moving to England.

I never imagined a town so dog-friendly as Windermere. It seemed as though half of the people in town owned a dog. Most businesses in town, pubs, outdoor restaurants and most stores, welcome and accommodate dogs.

I noticed that everyone walks, from one end of town to the other. This healthy habit is offset by the fact that so many of the British we saw, from teens to the elderly, smoked cigarettes. The last time I saw such so many people sucking on cigarettes was America in the 1960s.

Pay toilets are a thriving business in England. When you see a sign that reads "Public Washroom," expect a 20 to 40 pence admission charge. One fancy (40p) washroom I visited had an automatic electronic door lock and timer. Seven minutes, and you're done. (I suspect an ejector seat is involved.) There was also an automatic hand washer that *washes* and dries your hands. I was frankly surprised that patrons were expected to wipe their own bums.

We took a nice, long boat tour of the largest lake one day and took a bus to Grasmere another day to see the area that William Wordsworth (Judy's favorite) lived in and wrote about.

Our favorite food discovery in Windermere, England was the "Vinegar Jones" fish and chip shop. They cook their fresh fish with the same kind of batter we grew up with in Massachusetts. They charge half as much as the fancier restaurants in town, offset a tiny bit by the 25p charge for each tiny packet of ketchup. During our one week stay, we ate there four times!

One evening, we had dinner in a local pub. I wasn't in the mood for beer so I ordered a Black Russian, which is simply vodka and coffee liquor. The young bartender had no idea what that was so the elder bartender confidently stepped in and said, "I've got this." He poured a shot of vodka into a glass of Pepsi Cola.

Lesson learned. I should have ordered a beer.

Overall, our week in the Lake District was awesome.

London is a typical big city but with some cool historic buildings, monuments, and bridges. We bought tickets for a "Hop-On, Hop-Off" bus. While buying the tickets, Judy told the ticket seller that she was looking forward to seeing Shakespeare's Globe Theatre. He offered to sell her a ticket for the tour for £14, so she bought one. I opted out, figuring that I would be happier taking photos in the surrounding area while she toured the museum. While Judy is a diehard Shakespeare fan, I always joke that I might appreciate Shakespeare more had he written in English.

We took lots of photos from the upper deck of that bus. My funniest photo was of a sign advertising "Vegan KFC".

When we reached the Globe Theatre, she showed her ticket to a guard at the gate who said, "There are no tours today. They are rehearsing for a play." She showed him her ticket. He asked who sold her the ticket and she told him the guy from the bus company did.

"Well, that was naughty!" he said.

Judy was crushed. This was the one thing in London that she most looked forward to. She was nearly in tears. The guard said, "I'll tell you what. I'll take you into the theatre myself. You can take all the pictures you'd like, and I'll tell you what I know about the theatre."

While Judy had a private tour of the theatre and a self-tour of the exhibit hall, I waited outside taking candid photos of people for about an hour and a half. At one point, the guard walked over to me carrying a shopping bag. "Can I get you a cup of tea or anything?" he asked. I declined. He opened the shopping bag and took out two t-shirts. "I felt bad for your wife so I managed to get her two t-shirts and one of our fleece jackets. See? They say, "Globe Theatre: SECURITY". Can I leave them with you?" I was so impressed with this guy.

After Judy left the Exhibit Hall, we talked with the guard, whose name was Mark. He expressed how important it was to him that tourists have an enjoyable time visiting London. Judy thanked Mark for turning what could have been her worst experience in England into the most memorable.

It was time to fly to India.

DELHI

Our incredible return trip to India began on a sour note. Delhi was largely a disaster. The "daughter" we were supposed to stay with met us at the airport and brought us to a hotel in a section of Delhi called Karol Bagh. She said that we would be more comfortable there.

We were confused. More than a year ago she had invited us to stay in one of the empty apartments above her family's home. She talked about the meals she planned to cook for us. Why did she decide to put us up in a hotel and not a very comfortable one at that? We decided she probably found a hotel that she could afford, so it wasn't worth commenting on.

She and her sister and dad took us to see a Dusshera celebration, as planned. That was fun to see. People on stage acted out the story of Lord Rama rescuing his wife, Sita, with the help of Hanuman, and defeating the evil Ravaan while fireworks exploded above the crowd. The celebration ended when they shot flaming arrows at Ravaan and we all watched his giant effigy burn.

Then we all went to their home where they cooked us a huge, delicious dinner. The atmosphere was friendly and polite, but reserved. The family watched us while we ate. When Judy asked if they were going to join us they said that they would eat later. We took some photos together. Then they sent us back to our hotel. We didn't see them again for four or five days.

Most American cell phones don't work in India, so we needed to get a new sim card for the mobile phone we bought in Kolkata in 2015. Judy went to a Vodaphone store. She was charged 950 rupees for the new sim card. The Vodaphone employee insisted on cash and didn't provide a receipt. It took four return visits to the Vodaphone store before we had a sim card that actually worked. What's worse is, the employee who sold Judy the card reported charging her 450 rupees for it and pocketed 500 rupees!

A week later, Judy called Vodaphone's corporate office while we were in Jaipur. After much argument, Vodaphone said that they would be happy to refund the 500 rupees, but the company wouldn't return it from their Jaipur store. We would have to fly back to Delhi to collect it! Being without a working phone for most of our time in Delhi was a significant problem, because we were unable to access the internet from our phone or call anyone for help.

One evening, we hired a tuk-tuk to bring us back to our hotel. The driver dropped us off in a dark alley and said we should walk straight ahead then turn right. After some pointless arguing, we followed his directions and walked the entire length of that street until it ended. There was no sign of our hotel, no street signs, and no way to call the hotel for directions. We walked through crowds for more than an hour. The sun had gone down hours ago. We asked many people for directions. Some didn't speak English, and those who did had never heard of our hotel.

This was so frustrating. The streets were thick with people and the sidewalks were overrun by vendors. We had enjoyed a fun evening with the Delhi Drum Circle on the other side of the city and now just wanted to get to our hotel room and collapse. We had no sense of which direction to go. We finally asked an out-door shoe merchant who promptly left his shoe stand and asked a nearby watch merchant for help.

They spent twenty minutes searching for our hotel on a smart-phone. With the help of a 14-year-old boy, they found it. As it turns out, we needed to turn left at the end of the alley, not right. After walking several more kilometers (about a mile and a half) we reached our hotel. Judy's anger toward and my disappoint-ment in our absent host was growing daily.

The Karol Bagh section of Delhi is interesting. The area is famous for shopping for wedding attire and accessories. The streets are filled with vendors selling all sorts of things. The first time Judy and I tried taking a walk, I was approached by six street vendors selling cheap sunglasses. They were relentless, walking with us for as much as half a block trying to make a sale. After days of this aggressive and annoying approach, I turned rude and pointed to the sunglasses I was wearing and said, "I already HAVE sunglass-es!" The guys selling belts got the same routine: "I already HAVE a belt!" A dozen guys offered to shine my shoes. "I'm wearing SNEAKERS!"

One of the vendors who approached us almost daily was selling maps of India. "Map of India! Very good map! Top Quality! No problems!"

"No problems?" What sort of "problem" might one expect in a map? Do some spell Delhi incorrectly? Is the state of Rajasthan

sometimes missing? This guy would follow us for a few hundred feet before abandoning his sales pitch.

We were also approached by more beggars here than we saw in the rest of our time in India. There are even babies and toddlers, with their mothers, who put their hands out for money. Each night, we tried to sleep despite the sound of street dogs fighting and crying out in pain. After five days in this seedy hotel, I received a message from the young woman who put us here: "The travel agent needs to be paid for the hotel. The rate is 1250 rupees per day."

We were expected to pay for the hotel? It was bad enough that every meal had to be purchased in restaurants outside the hotel. The hotel cost was going to put us even further over budget. We hadn't even seen our "hosts" since the day we arrived!

This trip was beginning to feel like a huge mistake. We were not living with a family. I was not spending the quality time I had looked forward to with the young woman to whom I had felt so close. I felt bad for having dragged Judy here, but she was more concerned about my disappointment.

My friend Archana lives in the United States but was now in Kota, Rajasthan, India, trying to resolve a visa problem. She sent me a message asking how we were doing. I told her the story of our Delhi visit. She was angry and said, "You don't call someone 'Paa' and then leave him alone in a city like Delhi!" She insisted we check out of our hotel the next morning. She would pay for our train fare to Kota, where we could stay with her and her family until we were due to travel to Jaipur.

I thanked her, but declined. We were scheduled to celebrate my birthday at a Delhi restaurant on Saturday. Ten of my Delhi area Quora/Facebook friends were planning to come. It was better that we stay and leave Delhi on Sunday as planned.

We did end up seeing our host one more time. She and her sister took us shopping in their neighborhood. I had known this young woman very well online and was looking forward to spending time talking with her. Instead, the time we spent was polite and superficial. I wanted to ask about the change in plan and why she didn't tell me in advance, but we were never in a position to have a real conversation.

We had a nice surprise from my friend, Darsika Somaiya, from Pune. Our itinerary made visiting Pune impossible, despite my having a few good friends there. Before we left home, the closest of those friends, Darsika, asked me what t-shirt size I wore. I explained that I don't really wear t-shirts and thanked her for the thought. Instead, she mailed a package to Delhi containing a beautiful sari, earrings, and a necklace for Judy, along with some onion-garlic masala for me.

Another nice surprise was hearing from my friend, Harsh Kamagouda. Harsh lives in Bangalore, which had put him on the list of young people I wouldn't get to meet. One night, he wrote me on Facebook, "You're in Delhi *now*? I'm in Delhi! Are you free to meet tomorrow?" The three of us had a really nice lunch together.

Harsh suggested we all go to visit Gurudwara Bangla Sahib, an enormous Sikh temple in Delhi. We hired an Ola Cab (India's version of Uber) and visited the temple.

Shoes have to be removed before entering temples, which is painful for those of us who need arch support. I left my socks on, which earned me an admonishment by a Sikh. Socks are also not allowed. Sheesh! This meant a trip back to the shoe check-in counter. Sikhs require that the visiting public wear head coverings in the temple, so they provide barrels full of head scarves for public use.

Once inside, the temple is breathtaking. I recall the colors white and gold everywhere. There was a kirtan (devotional singing and chanting to music) going on, so we sat on the floor and listened for a while. Back at home there is a Sikh ashram in nearby Espanola, New Mexico. I once drummed for a large concert they held. I know Sikhs to be warm-hearted, service-oriented people, and the Sikhs at the Gurudwara Bangla Sahib are the same. They were consistently friendly and welcoming. Unlike some temples, photography was allowed inside this one.

After our visit to the Gurudwara Bangla Sahib, Harsh suggested we visit the Lotus Temple, which is a Bahá'í House of Worship that serves as the Mother Temple of the Indian subcontinent. It is open to people of all faiths. The 112-foot high building consists of 27 concrete and marble "petals" in the shape of a lotus and is an architectural wonder.

The staff is dedicated to keeping everyone in line and moving. There were more stairs involved than my arthritic knees wanted to deal with, but I survived it. Once inside the temple, which is large enough to seat 1300 people and hold a total of 2500, the sense of peacefulness was striking. We sat for some time before joining the line to exit.

Harsh treated us to fresh coconut milk. A coconut vendor whacks the coconut hard with a huge machete then inserts a straw for drinking. It was delicious. After spending such a great day with Harsh, he ordered an Ola Cab to take us all back to our hotel. As soon as the driver entered Karol Bagh, he pulled over to let us out claiming that the area was "too congested" to drive us to our hotel. He was not willing to approach our hotel from the less-congested side, and left us nowhere near our hotel. He was done. Period. Once again, no one had heard of our hotel. Despite the fact that we were now with a friend who spoke Hindi, the three of us were lost for more than an hour before we found it.

I talked with my friend, Ashish Khatri, who lives just outside Delhi. He knew some drivers and said he would try to find one for hire on a full-day or half-day basis, which he did within about an hour. The price was reasonable, but Ashish warned that the driver's English was very limited. We decided to pass. Being driven by someone we couldn't communicate with seemed like a potentially bad idea. Because Ashish works a night shift, meeting him was impossible.

We gave up on tuk-tuks and Ola Cabs and learned to ride the Metro subway system. There, again, we found people rude and inconsiderate. Men occupied the women's section of the Metro trains. Young people played with their smartphones seated in the section designated for elders and disabled people. Only twice in a dozen or more train rides did someone offer me their seat; both times it was middle-aged women. Otherwise, we stood holding handrails in trains that were often so crowded that we couldn't move two inches in any direction.

One afternoon, we had lunch with Nipanjana's niece, Riya Haldar. We met this beautiful nineteen-year-old woman at Nipanjana's wedding in 2015. Riya had taken Judy under her wing at the wedding, spent time explaining the sequence of events, and anticipated her every need. Judy says that Riya treated her like a celebrity. Though she's from Kolkata, Riya now attends college in Delhi, so we invited her to lunch. After hours of conversation, we came away impressed with the intelligence and depth of feeling of this young woman who is majoring in Japanese Studies.

We went to a huge shopping mall, Connaught Place, where Judy purchased two beautiful women's tunics called kurtis. While she was being fitted for alterations at the clothing shop, I waited downstairs for her where the store manager and the store owner were watching the news on television. They told me there had just been a sniper attack in Las Vegas, Nevada. Both of them were convinced that the sniper must be a Muslim. I told them, "I'll bet it turns out to be a crazy white person." We discussed world affairs and other topics.

The store owner placed a phone call. A while later, someone showed up with a paper bag from which the two men each took a five inch round dinner pastry called kachoris. They offered me the third one, which I declined. The store owner insisted that he had intentionally ordered the third one for me, and then handed it to me with a dish of curry for dipping this delicacy. It was delicious. Judy came downstairs and joined in the conversation.

When I finished my kachoris, the store manager suggested that I drink the last of the curry sauce, which is something I might do at home. It was great getting a go-ahead to enjoy it with these guys.

A Few Interesting Facts and Observations:

1. Clothing stores in India offer free alterations. In fact, the store manager I mentioned above told Judy, "Size is *my* problem, not *your* problem." You would never find this in US stores. Something fits or it doesn't. Buy it or don't buy it. If you need alterations, find and pay a tailor.

2. Even by India's standards, Delhi is crowded. In our home state of New Mexico, the average population density is 17 people per square mile. In our city of Santa Fe, the population density is 75 people per square mile. In contrast, Delhi has a population density of 29,600 people per square mile!

3. Judy watches a lot of BBC television, and I watch lots of Indian cinema. In England, I often had trouble understanding the British accent. Judy always understood perfectly what Brits were saying. In India, Judy struggled with the Indian accent at first. I always understood Indians. It became a joke between us, each of us translating English for the other.

The day before my birthday, many of my online friends wrote to tell me that they were sick, or had to work, or had classes. One friend thought we were meeting at the restaurant at a different time. When the time came for my birthday gathering, Judy and I sat alone for nearly thirty minutes at a long table reserved for ten people. Thankfully, my friends Rachna Jha and Shivanshi Singh Rathaur showed up and we had the best time! We spent four hours at the restaurant eating, talking and getting to know one another.

We had fun learning to eat pani puris, which is a hollow, round, crispy, deep-fried 2 ½" puri (fried pastry) filled with flavored water, chickpeas, potato and spices. When I popped one in my mouth, the liquid was released making it impossible to talk or open my mouth until it was swallowed.

Meanwhile, my Delhi "daughter" neither showed up, nor even wished me a Happy Birthday online. In fact, I haven't heard from her since. The hotel had already been booked before we landed in Delhi, so we couldn't have done or said anything offensive to make them decide against our staying in their home. Perhaps at the last minute, for whatever reason, her parents had changed their minds about us staying with them. Perhaps they found renters for the upstairs apartment. I have written to her asking what happened but have received no response. My biggest disappointment is that, after more than a year of planning, someone I felt so close to would change our mutual plans without informing us and then not offer an explanation.

We had some nice moments in Delhi but could have fit them into two days. It was the only visit that went sour. We joked that the next time we visit Delhi, it will be only at the airport changing planes to go somewhere else. Based solely on the experiences of this trip, Delhi became our least favorite city in India.

JAIPUR

Jaipur was already our favorite city in India. We flew there from Delhi via Air India. Our luggage weighed more than the baggage allowance — bear in mind we had packed for six weeks away from home — but Air India was kind enough to let it slide with no punitive charges. We had a reservation at a Radisson Hotel for our first week there. The plan was to stay with Nandita Sudha Tiwari and her sister Amrita Sudha Tiwari and their family for four days afterward. Instead, the two young women were already planning to take care of us soon after we checked in to our hotel.

This was a welcomed feeling after our experience in Delhi.

They met us at our hotel where we chatted for hours. I have always been impressed with Nandita, based on a year and a half's worth of online conversations. A physics major, Nandita is assertive, eloquent, quick-thinking, passionate, and beautiful with a natural elegance. It's no wonder she recently earned the Miss Rajasthan title. In December, she competed for the title of Miss India Khadi.

Nandita has been the online friend who always made me aware of women's social issues in India. This meeting was no exception. While we discussed women's issues and religion, Judy conversed with Nandita's older sister, Amrita. While Nandita and I were comfortable with each other through our extensive online connection, Judy and Amrita talked just as easily with each other, as if they had the same benefit of familiarity. The sisters announced that we were invited to dine at their house that night and suggested we arrive there at around 9:00 PM.

This was our introduction to the fact that families in India dine much later than Judy and I do. In the US, we eat breakfast early, lunch early, with dinner being over by 6:00 pm. In India, an elaborate breakfast is prepared when the cook gets up. Lunch is usually served in mid-afternoon. Dinner may happen anytime between 8:00 PM and 11:00 PM. I saw a dinner restaurant that didn't even open until 7:30 in the evening. We adjusted our eating schedules without much difficulty.

I faced several challenges regarding food. I had trouble convincing our host family moms that I don't eat breakfast. They couldn't understand that concept and did their best to entice me to eat something in the morning. Another difficulty was the fact that I actually eat less than it looks like I do. Our host moms might assume that I didn't like the food they prepared. I started alerting our host moms of my eating habits before they served us our first meal so they wouldn't think I didn't enjoy the food.

In fact, I loved the food! During our stay in Jaipur we got to eat home-cooked foods such as pulaav, aloo patta gobhi sabzi, daal, daal ki pakodi and chutney, paav bhaji, upmaa, daal bafla, daal dhokli, chapati, shrikhand, and wheat halwa.

My third food issue is that Judy loves bread and bready products, and I don't. Indians tend to eat all their meals with roti, chapati, paratha, naan, or other flat, round bread, using them to scoop up their food. Judy loved chapati so much that the moms taught her how to make it. She makes it all the time now. Most moms couldn't imagine why I would pass up bread at mealtime.

I expected to struggle with thirty-three days of the vegetarian diet, but didn't. I ate such good home-cooked food that I didn't miss meat . . . much. Before this trip, I joked to Nishchay that, after eating vegetarian for so many weeks, their local chickens wouldn't be safe around me.

By the time my poop was the color of curry, it seemed like a good time to have a non-veg lunch. I had previously found a Burger King in Delhi where they served a "Mutton Whopper," which tastes exactly like an American Whopper. An internet search revealed an address for a Burger King in Jaipur. We hired a car and off we went. I ordered a Mutton Whopper and Judy ordered the vegetarian burger.

When I ordered the Mutton Whopper in Delhi, I chose the one described as "spicy", which turned out to be a big disappointment. They made it spicy by adding a layer of broken tortilla chips onto the sandwich. C'mon. No chips of any kind belong inside a burger! And tortilla chips don't make a burger spicy; they make it crunchy. Yuck! I picked out every last bit. So, in Jaipur, I specified no tortilla chips in my Mutton Whopper. Call me fussy but, as much as I enjoy popcorn and ice cream, I don't want to find *those* in my burger either.

End of burger rant. My Mutton Whopper tasted great. During our time in India, I ate non-veg only three times. Our vegetarian meals were that good.

I found it interesting that most of the dishes we ate in people's homes are not available in our local Indian restaurants. In the US, menu selections are often limited to tandoori, fifty variations of curry, and naan bread. If I could stop at my local Indian restaurant and order dhokla, raj kachori, dal (not the soup), palak paneer, or egg curry, I would eat there three times a week!

Enough said about food for now. It's making me hungry.

Our hotel was unwilling to call us a cab to go to Nandita and Amrita's home, but they would supply a driver for about six times the cost, which we weren't happy about. We stepped outside hoping to find a cab or an auto rickshaw with no luck. We returned to the hotel and agreed to pay their ridiculous price.

Our driver got completely lost despite stopping to ask for direction no less than eight times. Judy managed to momentarily get a Wi-Fi signal on her phone and called the Tiwari house. Amrita showed up on her "Scooty" (a motor scooter marketed for women) and led our driver to her home. That was the first and last time we used the hotel's high-priced car service.

Our Indian phone was an outdated, clam shell, non-smart phone so we couldn't download the Uber app. After that incident, Nandita or Amrita took ownership of our travel needs and ordered Uber cabs for us anytime we needed to go somewhere.

Once at the house, we met Sudha, their mom, and Shreenath, their younger brother. Shree is a pretty cool guy. He works for a sales and marketing company in China, but was home due to a visa problem. He is a gentle, funny, and attentive person. Judy wore an Indian kurti and Shree made a point of complimenting her. Nandita laughed and said he was a big flirt.

Shree asked if I played the guitar. I wondered why he would even guess that and told him I did more than thirty years ago. He handed me a guitar with a missing string and insisted that I play. Judy and I sang my old comedy song, "Do the Mushroom". We did one verse and one chorus and ended it. I was seriously out of practice, but the family was delighted! Judy played her Native American-style flute during our visit. The family was enchanted with the unusual tone which was so new to them. What a joy to share our music with people who were sharing so much with us!

Indians usually sit on the floor to eat at home. This is considered a healthy practice even by today's Western medical community. Since there is no need for a dining room table, we were often served meals on stainless steel platters on our bed. The food was great, as was the conversation. At the end of the night they ordered an Uber cab to take us back to our hotel.

Each day, Nandita checked to see what we were doing. She arranged to take us shopping at the Hawamahal Bazaar later that week. She told us that her aunt invited us to dinner at her home the next night, and we all met there. We met their Aunt Ritu Joshi, Uncle Suman, and their cousins Harsha and Devendra. We enjoyed another great meal. It turned out that Harsha was studying to be a psychologist. We talked about psychology and I told her about my last book, "MiXED NUTS".

The family was dealing with their very sick four-year-old dog "Google" who the vet expected wouldn't last the week. He died several days later and Harsha wrote a tribute on Facebook that made me teary:

"I remember convincing everyone to bring you home. You were so small and cuddly with your tiny paws and soft fur. You bounced around the room with eyes flashing and ears flopping. Making a mess of the house and chewing everything in sight became a passion, and when I scolded you, you just put your head down and looked up at me with those innocent eyes as if to say, "I'm sorry, but I'll do it again as soon as you are not watching". Whenever I woke up early to study you always tempted me to sleep my "little snoring beast". You were the reason why every birthday cake became so important.

As you got older, you protected me, always waiting for me to return home and welcoming me with that wagging tail. I knew I could always count on you. You led me from patience to love and then loss but every moment with you was worth it. You will always be my first baby. R.I.P. I hope you get an amazing next life."

Worse yet, their puppy Leo died the same week with symptoms of the same condition, which local veterinarians were unable to diagnose. We unexpectedly lost our own dog Dala earlier in August, and were heartbroken for their pain.

~:~:~:~:~:~:~:~:~:~:~:~

Judy and I were both determined to return from India with new kurtis and kurtas. We planned to meet Nandita and Amrita in front of the Hawa Mahal. While we waited for them, a man with a severely deformed leg using a crutch approached me selling post-cards. Not needing postcards, I declined, and he went away.

I watched him approach other people. I saw him smile when a child did something cute. I watched him laugh when something funny happened. Observing him, I had to admit I really liked him. This was a good-hearted individual. I approached him and told him I'd like to give him some money to help him out. He smiled, shook his head and said with sincerity and gratitude, "No. I'm happy." He was willing to earn a living by selling postcards and refused a handout. In retrospect, I wish I had bought his postcards.

Nandita and Amrita arrived and brought us across the street to meet their Uncle Sudhir at his jewelry shop where he sells beauti-ful precious gems. I bought a 22-carat *star ruby*, which is the rarest type. Light reflecting off of one creates a six-pointed star on its surface. He sold it to me for the equivalent of $22 USD. As a gift, Sudhir had Judy and me each choose a smaller star ruby. Judy reasoned that since Sudhir is a jeweler, it made sense to have rings made with our rubies. Now we both have a sweet memory of Sudhir's generosity.

Uncle Sudhir then brought us shopping at the Hawamahal Bazaar. Since his shop was one of the oldest shops in the bazaar, every shopkeeper knew and respected him. Whenever Judy saw something she was interested in buying, the dialogue went like this:

Shopkeeper: "That'll be 4000 rupees."

Sudhir: "And how much with my discount?"

Shopkeeper: "Make that 3500 rupees."

Sudhir: "But you'll be willing to take 3000 rupees?"

Judy was able to find a few kurtis. However, since India doesn't produce many guys my size, finding kurtas for me in these small outdoor shops proved to be a challenge. Apparently, there is a big difference between size XL in the United States and size XL in India. I joked that India's XL-size tunics are small enough for me to use as a hat.

Nandita told me that her Aunt Ritu owns a business that makes custom clothing and employs a full-time tailor. The next day, we were invited to return to Aunt Ritu's house for dinner and a kurta fitting. Ritu's husband, Suman, helped me choose fabrics and co-ordinating trim while the tailor measured me for my new kurtas. Less than a week later I had five new fancy lined Rajasthani kurtas and a traditional jacket at a very reasonable cost. I probably got the family discount.

Nandita and Amrita did everything they could to ensure that everything went smoothly for us. The two of them made us feel loved and cared for. Whenever we thanked them, which was often, their reply was, "Family doesn't need to say thank you."

I recall one evening when Amrita and Nandita gathered around the bed showing Judy their various outfits. That scene looked and *felt* like family.

My conversations with Nandita are memorable. Hindu scripture dictates that a woman is "impure" during her menstrual period and forbidden to enter temples. I found it interesting that so many world religions including Christianity, Judaism, and Islam also consider a menstruating woman spiritually unclean and have specific doctrines limiting her spiritual activity. It's also interesting to note that in Buddhism and Sikhism a woman's menstrual cycle is seen as a natural (God-given) process that in no way affects a woman's purity or spirituality.

Nandita found it hard to believe that the Hindu gods and goddesses were uncomfortable with a woman's biology. I had to admit that any mystery, awkwardness, or discomfort about such a natural process sounded suspiciously like the reaction of the men and not gods. She talked about the process of purchasing feminine hygiene products in India, where the products are often placed discreetly in black bags or double bags. "Do they think I'm ashamed of my own biology? Ashamed of being a woman?" She complained that, though one hears a lot of talk about equality for women in India, the reality has a long way to go. Nandita also pointed out the fact that sexually-conservative India was once a liberal culture as evidenced by the Kama Sutra and Tantric practices.

Nandita is a force to be reckoned with.

In my many years of enjoying Bollywood movies, I noticed that the main characters were always fair-skinned while darker-skinned Indians were cast in the roles of servants, sidekicks, friends, and idiots. I mentioned this to an Indian friend once who immediately assured me that I was mistaken. He felt I saw a pattern where none existed.

When we were simply online friends getting to know one another, Nandita shared several articles that supported my observation. Skin-lightening creams, skin bleaching, and chemical peels have become a multi-billion rupee market in India, endorsed by the darker-skinned celebrities who use those cosmetics and procedures. Today, there are some Bollywood stars and models who are speaking out against what they consider to be a subtle form of racism. A movement called "Dark is Beautiful" began in 2009.

Nandita is, for me, the voice of Indian social conscience, especially where Indian women are concerned.

As I mentioned in my 2015 travelogue, traffic in India is initially unsettling to a westerner. There are very few marked lanes, cars drive on the left, center, or right, and everyone plays "chicken". Whoever blinks first relinquishes the right of way. The pecking order appears to be: large trucks, buses, small trucks, cars, tuk-tuks, motorcycles, motor scooters, bicycles, pedestrians — in that order. When we walked with Nandita and Amrita, they would take our hand and guide us across the street.

One evening, Judy and I took a walk by ourselves and were returning to our hotel on foot. To get to our hotel we had to cross a ridiculously busy street of six lanes with a constant flow of traffic. We waited and waited for a break in the traffic, but there was none in sight. Suddenly, an old man appeared who looked to be well in his eighties. He came up beside me, took my hand and proceeded to cross the street with the two of us in tow while I held Judy's hand. He assertively signaled at the vehicles, which slowed down for us and allowed for a safe crossing. I thanked him in Hindi, and he waved and went on his way. It struck me funny that a frail old guy at least twenty years older than me had just helped us cross a street. At least he wasn't also blind!

There was a warmth in Jaipur that was unchanged since 2015.

Here is something interesting:

Many Indians in India think that "vegan" means the same as vegetarian. They are often surprised when I tell them that vegans eat no animal byproducts whatsoever, even those that are given freely such as honey and dairy products.

Indians have been using honey as a sweetener and in Ayurvedic medicine for over 5000 years. Hindus once considered honey a food of the gods and it was an integral part of wedding ceremonies.

A non-dairy diet means no ghee or paneer and no yogurt, which is the basis of most Indian curry. It also means no lassis. Chai is out since it is made with water and milk. Chhena, which is used in many Indian sweets, is also a dairy product. Dozens of basic ingredients in Indian foods are made by boiling down milk. With 75 million dairy farms, India has been the top milk-producing country worldwide since 1997. Unlike the US, India's dairy products are not from cows but from buffalo.

When I explained the difference between vegan and vegetarian to one of my Indian friends, she said that Indians would starve on such a diet.

After our week at the Radisson City Center Hotel, we moved into Nandita and Amrita's house for the remainder of our time in Jaipur. Though October in northern India is normally mild, October 2017 was unseasonably hot, averaging 31celcius or 88 farenheit during the day. We were given a comfortable room with a window-mounted air cooler and an attached bathroom with a western toilet. Amrita helped us find an ATM that would accept our American bank cards and took us grocery shopping. Nandita helped us ship some books back home so we could avoid paying fees for the extra weight as we continued our airline travel.

I was itching to take a solo walk around the neighborhood. Everyone argued that it was too hot or that I might get lost, but I was vehement. I reluctantly agreed to take a phone with me just in case. (I'm notorious for *never* carrying my cell phone with me.)

It was an enjoyable walk. I brought my camera to take some candid photos of people, and found a steep curb to sit on as I observed the neighborhood.

A vendor, about forty feet to my right, was selling something I couldn't see, while to my left, a young girl swept in front of her house with a straw broom. Some kids were playing together. Two men were talking with a vendor across the street. A few women were coming in and out of their houses. With a gesture, a nearby vendor offered me a seat beside him. I thanked him in Hindi and declined. I had a better view here. A woman across the street offered me water. A second woman across the street offered me chai. I took photos of the two women in their colorful outfits.

It wasn't a busy street so, as I sat on the curb, only an occasional vehicle drove past. A motorcycle went by and the driver looked at me the very second I looked at him. It was the tailor who measured me for my kurtas! He drove by too fast for us to wave or acknowledge each other in any way, but we saw the recognition on each other's faces. I thought to myself, in a city of three million people on the other side of the world, what are the odds of my knowing someone driving by? Apparently, when he got to Ritu's shop, he expressed the same surprise at seeing me sitting by myself on a curb in a random neighborhood.

A man approached me with his pre-teen son. He gestured to his son as if encouraging him to speak:

Boy: "Where from?"

Rick: "USA. Where are you from? India?" (grinning)

Boy: "Yes".

Rick: "Jaipur is my favorite part of India! What's your name?"

Boy: "Ashish"

Rick: "Ashish? I have a friend named Ashish!"

Boy: "Your name?"

Rick: "My name is Rick."

Boy: (nods) "Rick"

Rick: "Can I take your picture, Ashish?"

Boy: (nods and smiles)

Rick: (Takes a picture and shakes Ashish's hand.) "It's a pleasure meeting you, Ashish!"

Boy: "You, too."

During this interaction, Ashish's father looked on proudly. I guessed that the boy had been learning English and had no one to practice with. I think it could be why his dad brought him over. The man sincerely thanked me without words.

Rick: "Bye Ashish!"

Boy: "Bye".

The Dad disappeared into a nearby house while Ashish joined his young friends down the street who I passed as I headed back to the house. I waved and said, "Bye Ashish!" The kids all stood there looking dumbfounded. Ashish waved and said bye. As I weaved my way through right and left turns, I heard several voices half a block behind me:

"Rick! Rick! Rick!"

I turned to see Ashish and ten of his friends in the street waving at me! I waved back vigorously.

Another half block down the street I heard it again:

"Rick! Rick! Rick!"

Again I turned to see them all waving enthusiastically. I waved back and grinned the rest of the way to the house.

I didn't get lost.

I got found.

One of the funniest things that happened while staying at Nandita's home took place the afternoon we heard what we thought was a smoke alarm go off. Judy checked the other room and saw that Sudha had lit some incense. She came back and said it was probably what triggered the smoke detector. The next afternoon we heard the smoke detector go off again. Judy mentioned hearing the "fire alarm" again and asked Nandita if everything was okay.

Nandita said "Fire alarm?" She began to chuckle and left the room. She returned ringing a small brass bell. She said, "My mother rings this each day when she says her prayers. You thought that this was a *fire alarm?*"

We all laughed.

We became accustomed to the early morning sound of vendors in the streets shouting out to potential customers — one selling fruits and vegetables, another picking up things to be recycled. I learned to imitate them pretty well and told everyone that some morning I planned to walk through the neighborhood yelling, "Bomada BAAAAY! Bomada BAAAAY!" I predicted that it would get people's attention because it *meant nothing* and *made no sense.* Sometimes a drummer playing a dhol drum (a very loud two-headed drum struck with long sticks) would come through the neighborhood and earn money by playing for people at their houses.

One morning we heard music and singing that seemed to be coming up our street. Judy asked if they were singing in anticipation of Diwali or celebrating a wedding.

"No, that's the garbage song!" replied Amrita. She explained that Prime Minister Modi started a clean-up program. The garbage truck plays the song to encourage people to bring out their garbage, so it can be picked up.

I lied and said I understood the Hindi lyrics perfectly. *"We're so happy picking up the trash... Whoops, there's a stinky bit! ...Whoa, there's a stinky bit!"*

One afternoon, Amrita took us shopping at a local market. No sign of ground cardamom, which I use to make homemade masala chai and lassis (an Indian yogurt drink). I did, however, find Diet Pepsi which isn't popular yet in India but was a welcome sight for me. I was beginning to miss the food, snacks, and drinks I sometimes enjoy at home. I also bought a small bag of potato chips and a package of Oreo cookies, which surprised Amrita. "Aren't those for kids?" she asked. To this big kid, Diet Pepsi, potato chips, and Oreos tasted like home.

Nandita wanted to take us out to dinner before we left Jaipur. The restaurant she had in mind made a mistake in the reservation and scheduled us for the evening we would already be gone. She tried unsuccessfully to reschedule. Then, she and Amrita planned to take us downtown where the Diwali lights would be lit all night, describing them as quite a spectacle. When we got into town via tuk-tuk, the lights were off. We discovered the next day that the power company employees went on strike and purposely cut the power to the Diwali lights in order to get everyone's attention. Nandita was frustrated that none of her plans was working out.

The next day, as we packed to leave, Nandita gave us a collage-type picture frame as a gift. At the bottom is the word "FAMILY". It is the absolute perfect gift. The frame now holds a photo of Judy and me wearing Rajasthani outfits, surrounded by pictures of each of our host families in India. It hangs in our home on a wall with our other family pictures.

KOTA

During our time in Delhi, my friend Archana Saurabh had asked that Judy and I check out of the Karol Bagh hotel stay with her in Kota. She later suggested we borrow a day or two from the Jaipur trip and that she would pay for our train tickets to Kota and then back to Jaipur as my birthday gift. I wasn't expecting to meet Archana and her family, so this was an offer I couldn't refuse.

At the time of our trip, Archana, her husband Saurabh Sagar, and their two-year-old son, Aadih, were living with her in-laws in Kota. They had returned temporarily from living and working in the United States and were awaiting Archana's new visa.

I knew that, if I were ever lucky enough to meet her, it would be an absolute joy. So, off we went.

The train ride from Jaipur to Kota took four hours. We rode comfortably in a 2AC car, which accommodates four people and is air conditioned. A man walked through the train periodically selling sandwiches. He spoke in a mixture of English with Hindi, so his vending call sounded like, "Hey cuddle diddle-diddle sandwiches!" I bought one mostly to see what the heck was in it. It was a small bit of cheese between two slices of bread. Cuddle diddle-diddle cheese, I suppose.

Archana and her father-in-law, Pawan, were waiting for us at the train station.

Knowing Archana from our chats and her photos online, I knew her smile. A glow emanated from that smile. I hugged Archana with all my heart and introduced Judy.

Pawan wasn't a very talkative guy, but he drove out of his way several times to show us sights that he thought we would enjoy. This is when I saw the *first* photogenic sunset of this India trip — across Kishore Sagar Lake. Now it was thrilling to capture a second stunning sunset in India! One of my favorite sunset shots is from a boat on the Ganges River taken during our 2015 trip to Kolkata.

Across Kishore Sagar Lake we could see a park that displays replicas of the Seven Wonders of the World in miniature. From where we stood, we could see the Taj Mahal, the Leaning Tower of Pisa, the Statue of Liberty, and more. It reminded me of the time when Judy and I were moving to Santa Fe, New Mexico from Yarmouth, Maine. We stopped in Rolla, Missouri for the night and visited a miniature version of Stonehenge known as "Stubby Stonehenge". Here, in Kota, one could see mini versions of Christ the Redeemer of Brazil, the Colosseum, the Great Pyramids, and the Eiffel Tower while saving a bundle on airfare!

We stopped at "Lovely Fruit Juice and Shake", which was a fond memory for Archana because she used to come here when she was a student.

I ordered a papaya shake with ice cream, because where else will I ever find a papaya shake with ice cream? It did not disappoint. Judy tries to limit her sugar intake, so she ordered a pineapple shake without the ice cream.

We drove past a large, round area in the middle of an intersection which had four gigantic carved elephants, each facing in one of the four directions. Archana explained that there was originally an eagle monument displayed there. A business located in the direction the eagle faced had failed, leading people to suspect that the eagle was to blame. Each time it was turned in a different direction another business failed. Convinced that the eagle monument was to blame, it was removed and replaced by the four elephants to avoid any further bad luck.

We met Archana's husband, Saurabh, and their son, Aadih, Saurabh's mother, Madhu, and others at the house. We were made to feel at home instantly and were shown to the only room that had air conditioning and a bathroom with a western-style toilet. We suspected that Archana and Saurabh had given up their room for us.

While Archana, Saurabh, Judy, and I were talking, I must have spoken enthusiastically about something because Archana turned to Saurabh and said, "Oh my God! He looks and sounds just how I pictured him!"

I knew what she meant. It was how I felt meeting her.

Dinner included the best dal (lentils) I have ever tasted. I'm accustomed to the "dal soup" served in Indian restaurants in America. This was more like dal stew, spicy and delicious with chunks of ingredients. I could have skipped every other dish put before me and filled up on this amazing dal. Today, it has become a staple in our home.

Kota is called "Education City" because it is the home of so many coaching institutes that prepare as many as 150,000 young people per year to take the rigorous Indian Institute of Technology (IIT) exams. The IIT is a group of 23 of the best public colleges in India. More than a million students compete for only 5000 seats. According to India's National Crime Records Bureau, Kota had 45 student suicides in 2014 alone.

There were lots of young people in town. The city had a small town atmosphere. We were borrowing a few days from our time in Jaipur, but I could have easily spent more time with Archana and her family in Kota.

The next morning, Saurabh drove us to the town of Bundi, a thousand-year-old city with a population of just under 100,000. We visited "Raniji ki Baori," a step well in Bundi. A step well is an ancient architectural form in India where a well was dug down to the water table and reached by descending a series of steps. The wells were used as reliable access to water and for social gatherings and religious ceremonies, since their subterranean depth made their temperatures considerably cooler than at ground level. Known as the "Queen's Step Well", this one was built in 1699 and is among the largest in the state of Rajasthan. The well is 150 feet (46 meters) deep and richly decorated with elaborate carvings.

After visiting the Raniji ki Baori, Saurabh drove us to see Garh
Palace (aka Bundi Palace). The streets of Bundi are quite narrow,
and the way to the palace requires many turns. Saurabh stopped
to ask locals for directions many times. He called this "using the
local GPS".

Bundi Palace was once described by Rudyard Kipling as "the
work of goblins rather than of men" because it appears to have
been carved from stone jutting unnaturally out of a green moun-
tainside. Famous for its wall and ceiling frescoes, the four hun-
dred-year-old palace is in need of some extensive restorative
work but remains photogenic. Seeing the palace requires walking
us steep roads and staircases.

A section of the palace is now a private hotel with an area where a
vendor sells jewelry. Despite this, the palace was worth the visit.
We were nearly at the highest level of the palace when I spotted a
very steep staircase. Deciding to give my knees a break, I told the
others to go on without me. I stayed and took photos.

This is when I met two young men named Sitaram and Prince.
They told me more about the palace, and I told them about our
current visit to India. Judy, Archana, and Saurabh looked down
from the upper level and saw me talking with them. Judy joked,
"By the time we get back to where Rick is, I wouldn't be surprised
to find him talking to a crowd of 20 people!"

(A week later, in the Triveni Art and Culture Museum in Ujjain,
Judy would snap a picture of me talking with a crowd of more
than 20 visitors from Gujarat. My life cracks me up.)

We had a scary moment driving through Kota. Saurabh's car was stuck in traffic with two bulls alongside in the street. The bulls began fighting violently just inches from the car! We all braced ourselves for impact, anticipating that one of the bulls would slam into the car. It didn't happen. The traffic moved and so did we.

On our final day in Kota, during our last meal at Saurabh's parent's home, we were served kachori, which is a thin deep-fried pastry ball with a spicy dal filling. Saurabh's mother, Madhu, who initially believed that westerners have no tolerance for spices, finally accepted that Judy and I *do* and risked including kachori with our lavish dinner. I would eat them every day if I could!

When it was time to leave, an entire contingent of family and neighbors stood in front of the house bidding us goodbye. Our train was scheduled to leave for Jaipur at six o'clock and was an hour late. Archana had tried to purchase 2AC seats on the train, but they were filled. The best seats available were 3AC with air-conditioning and seating for eight instead of four. The beds were not made to accommodate tall people.

This trip was a wonderful, unexpected gift. When saying goodbye to Archana at the train, I told her, "If I say thank you one more time, I'll start to cry."

I meant it.

UJJAIN

Located on the eastern bank of the Kshipra River, Ujjain (pronounced OO-jain) is the fifth largest city in the Indian state of Madhya Pradesh, often referred to as "MP" by Indians. More than 2700 years old, it is considered one of the seven holy cities of India. One of its claims to fame is that it was where Lord Krishna studied under the tutelage (gurukul) of saint Sandipani Muni.

We flew from Jaipur to Indore via Jet Airways, who were less tolerant of our luggage weighing more than the 14-kilo allotment than Air India had been. They charged us an extra 3000rs ($47.00 USD). We agreed to stick with Air India for domestic flights next time.

My "son" Nishchay Maheshwari and his 11-year-old sister, Arya, met us at the Indore Airport with a hired driver who took us to Nishchay's home in Ujjain. It was good to finally meet Nishchay face-to-face after many hours of online conversations. Nishchay is best described as innocent and gentle with a dedication to his studies and a real talent for music. He is a loving son and brother. Following a tight, long overdue hug, we talked throughout the hour-long car ride. Arya, who was sitting up front with Nishchay, shyly looked back many times to sneak looks at Judy and me.

When we reached Nishchay's home, a large group of people was gathered in front of the house. I instantly recognized his mother, Susmita, who is also one of my Facebook friends, as well as his father, Akshay, who I had seen in photos. I didn't know the rest of the people, but everyone immediately began performing a ceremony known as puja, showering us with blessings, touching our feet, anointing our foreheads with a tilaka of red vermillion paste, rotating a tray clockwise in front of us, and tossing yellow flower petals over our heads. I previously thought of a puja as a Hindu form of ritual prayer to the gods. After some research, I discovered that a puja is sometimes performed to honor and celebrate the presence of special guests. I have never experienced a more surprising or more moving reception.

We were introduced to each person, and although it was all a blur at the time, we got to know most of them in the days to come, as the family often brought us around to meet neighbors and relatives.

Our room had an attached bathroom with a western toilet and a huge portable air cooler which made it very comfortable.

I warned Susmita that I don't eat as much as I look like I eat. After a delicious meal, she commented in Hindi that I eat less than her 11-year-old daughter. She amended that a few days later, saying that I eat less than their parrot!

When it was time for prayers, it was assumed that we would take part. The family invited us to the Krishna shrine set up in the far end of the kitchen where Arya knelt and performed the nightly puja. It was quite a beautiful and moving ceremony that ended with the family singing a song in Hindi. They encouraged us to join them in the last part of the song, "Hare Krishna, Hare

Krishna, Krishna Krishna, Hare Hare, Hare Rama, Hare Rama..."
I've known those words since my teens but I've never had to sing
them this fast before!

It was our first night in Ujjain, and the inclusiveness made me
feel like I was already a part of this beautiful family.

Judy and I gave gifts to everyone, as we did for each of our host
families. I designed and made 25 pairs of Indian-style earrings for
the women, we gave each family a container of my homemade
masala (spice mixture) for making chai, and we gave bracelets to
some of the women along with other accessories. We gave each
of the host family dads a package of dried mango slices coated
with sugar and New Mexico red chile powder.

Nishchay's dad, Akshay, has a very good sense of humor and a
big, memorable laugh. He listened to my funny stories and remembered them. When he showed us the various elements of
their Krishna shrine, he lifted the brass bell and announced, "Fire
alarm bell". At one dinner, while he poured some ghee over one
of my dishes, he brought his face close to mine, grinned, and said,
"Indian Oil".

While Judy and I had quickly become accustomed to the difference in dining hours and the vegetarian dishes, the one thing
Judy missed was coffee in the morning. Our hosts served chai in
the morning. The first morning at Nischay's home, Susmita said
"Good Morning! . . . Coffee?" Judy's face lit up and she said "Coffee!" and gave Susmita a big hug. Susmita and Judy laughed and

the offer of coffee each morning was followed by giggles, remembering that first morning.

Judy was fond of telling Nishchay's mom that she was "blessed by Annapurna", the Hindu Goddess of food and nourishment. Susmita would serve us food and then quietly notice which foods we seemed to prefer. This helped her decide what foods to prepare for the next meal. As a result, each meal was even better than the last! She is an amazing cook. Some of the dishes she cooked that week included Besan Pakodas, Bhindi Ki Sabzi, Besan Bhajiya In Siders, Aloo Tamatar Ka Saag, Dal Makhani, Rice Jeera, Laccha Paratha, Chapati, Gujiya, Papadi, Mathri, Dalmoth, Besan K Ladoo, Anarsa, and Barfi.

While I'm singing her praises, I'll add that Susmita also earned my "Prettiest Smile in Ujjain Award". Her entire face lights up when she smiles.

An unexpected surprise from Nishchay came when he announced that I would be cooking my vegetable biryani for the family. I had posted a picture of it on Facebook that he remembered.

Ummm . . . in someone else's kitchen? With someone else's knives and cookware? I'll have to buy supplies. Just what sort of veggies were even available in Indian grocery stores? Apprehensively, I agreed to do it. Nishchay took me to a grocery store on the back of his motor scooter, and I found enough fresh veggies to make the biryani taste good and look colorful.

I confess to be one of those people who doesn't want anyone in the kitchen while I'm cooking. It's not that I'm anti-social; it's just that I tend to do things with laser-like focus. It is one of the benefits from several years of practicing Transcendental Meditation in my late teens and early 20s. My head got quiet and my ability to focus intensified. How would I delicately ask Susmita to stay out of her *own* kitchen — especially after she offered to help?

My request seemed strange, but I was left to work alone. When the biryani was done, we kept it warm while Susmita took back her kitchen. She cooked Nishchay's favorite dish, Palak Paneer, which is a delicious combination of finely-chopped spinach, large chunks of paneer, and spices. Everyone treated the meal like a formal dinner, dressed up and seated at the rarely-used dining room table. The two dishes tasted delicious together!

A Few More Interesting Facts and Observations:

1. I often saw young women walking around or riding their bikes or scooters wearing beautiful scarves wrapped around their heads, allowing only their eyes to be visible through the scarf. I assumed they were Muslim, wearing fancy hijabs. It turns out that Indian women wear scarves like this to protect from the sun, to keep from breathing polluted air, and to protect their skin from dust

2. Touching feet is a very old Indian tradition. It is done as a show of respect to one's elders and also as a way of asking for that elder's blessing. To respond by placing one's hand on the younger person's head is a way of saying that he or she *has* your blessing.

3. Arranged marriages are still the primary route to marriage in

India, but "love marriages" have been steadily gaining popularity, especially in urban areas.

4. India's divorce rate is only 1%, but rising, and is higher in urban areas. Traditionalists believe that the increased number of divorces reflects the breakdown of society, while others believe it indicates a healthy new empowerment of women who initiate 80% of the divorces in India.

5. The consumption of beef is not considered an offense in the states of West Bengal or Kerala. In fact, in Kerala, beef accounts for about half of the total meat consumed.

6. Speaking of Kerala, here are some interesting facts:

a) Kerala has the highest literacy rate (94%), the lowest population growth, the lowest poverty rate, the lowest homeless rate, the lowest homicide rate, the lowest infant mortality rate, and the highest life expectancy of all the Indian states.

b) Because it's a matriarchal society where the women inherit and mothers are the head of the household, Kerala women enjoy a higher standing and influence in society. Kerala is also the only state in India where the women outnumber the men.

c) The per capita consumption of alcohol in Kerala was so high that it was prohibited in 2014. Only when illegal drug use increased and the tourist trade decreased was the prohibition recently lifted.

Nishchay's sister, Arya was precious. Smart, pretty, talented, graceful, and with a depth of heart that was unmistakable, a rare combination for an eleven-year-old. There was an event at school that only occurs every four years. Arya wanted to be the announcer for this event, but the school administrators regarded her as too young for the job. Arya took pride in the fact that she had not yet invoked Nishchay's name despite his excellent record and reputation with the school. Not to be brushed off so easily, she announced, "I'm Nishchay Maheshwari's sister, and I can do this."

She got the job.

She even did the speech for us which I videotaped. She also did a Bollywood dance, and I videotaped that, too. Her facial expressions and graceful hand gestures were amazing. Days later, when I complimented her on her dancing, she shrugged off my compliment as though it was undeserved.

We all visited a Krishna temple in Ujjain. It was my favorite of the Ujjain temples. When the kirtan players began, I left Nishchay, Judy, and Arya and moved to the other side of the temple so I could see the kirtan musicians and the dancers who accompanied them.

While everyone in the temple looked forward, I faced the rear watching the kirtan players. Arya noticed that I had moved to the other side of the temple. She joined me, took my hand, and pointed out the different statues of Krishna while explaining the stories behind them. Her interest and knowledge was impressive. The next evening, she sat beside me and showed me a book about Lord Krishna, telling me the story behind each picture from Krishna's birth through his childhood into adulthood.

Arya and Judy spent hours playing games together. Weeks after we returned home, Arya chatted with me on Facebook and quizzed me about Lord Krishna. I got one out of two questions correct. She said that she would prepare even tougher questions for the next day. (Those weren't the tough questions?)

How could I not love this girl?

I won't go into how I met Nishchay. He covered that nicely in the Foreword. I will say that he has a huge heart, a ton of determination, and is a natural musician. Like my own son, Mike, if you hand him a tuba, a violin, or any instrument, he will make music for you in less than an hour.

Nishchay's dream is to become a chartered accountant. When we first met, he was enrolled in a program that prepares students for an exam only thirty percent pass. He passed, which made him eligible to study for the next exam that typically has a seven percent pass rate. He rented an apartment near home, received coaching, and studied more than twelve hours a day. He only returned home to eat and sleep. This went on for a year. He would write to me when he felt discouraged and worried that he would burn out. When I suggested he take breaks, he told me that he took a five-minute break every four hours. Three hundred people took the exam. Only fifteen passed, and Nishchay, at nineteen, was one of them.

Education is tough in India. Because of the population, competition for good jobs is stiff. It seems that India's education system eliminates *average* students and focuses on the above-average students. Although the country has a rich history of artistic contributions, today's India does little to encourage young people who are interested in entering the arts. In the United States, a four-year, B-average college student can become CEO of a corporation. In India, one may need an MBA or a PhD just to land an entry-level job in a desired field.

Nishchay plays keyboards and guitar. After hearing Judy play flute on YouTube videos, he began learning to play the flute. Judy gave him a beautiful Native-American flute unobtainable in India. Nishchay bought her an Indian transverse flute as thanks.

The three of us improvised music together most days: Nishchay on guitar, Judy on native flute, and me playing a conga drum, which a local music store let us borrow for the week at no rental cost. We had planned to perform a concert for friends, relatives, and neighbors on the roof of their house, but Akshay realized that moving the concert indoors would yield better sound.

Akshay loves to sing and he's good at it. He has an audio setup that allows him to sing into a microphone while recorded music plays in the background. He raises one foot to a chair, lifts the microphone to his mouth and sings very serious and moving Bollywood songs. Arya had drawn a family portrait in school. Under her dad's picture she wrote, "my dad is the best singer." Akshay was our opening act.

Many people gathered in the living room/family room. Nishchay, Judy, and I played several improvisations together. Most pieces started out beautiful and melodic thanks to Judy's flute playing. Judy would then drop out as Nishchay and I sped things up, which excited the crowd. At times the entire audience would clap their hands to our beat. Judy and I sang "Do the Mushroom" together, this time getting through the entire song. The audience loved it. I wish they could have seen us perform this thirty plus years ago!

At the end of the concert a woman approached Judy and discreetly handed her an envelope. She told Judy how much she enjoyed our music. We opened the envelope before we turned in for the night. It contained a 100 rupee bill.

Several people let me know how much they loved watching me play and how they loved the expressions on my face when I play. Many people invited us to visit their homes. Judy also heard from guests who were fascinated by her flutes. Native American-style flutes simply don't exist in India except for Nishchay's. Our little concert was so well received that other people called the next morning asking us to play a repeat performance. We all agreed.

This time it was standing room only with twice as many people, including the owner of Akshay's company. Some people brought us flowers. We asked Arya to announce us. In a booming and confident voice accompanied by sweeping hand gestures she began:

"Good afternoon, everyone! Today, I want to welcome you all to be a part of this auspicious and wonderful event..."

Our Encore Concert was a huge success. We had several guest singers including Akshay, Arya, Yash, and Darchana. Ayush played two Bollywood songs on a melodica. People stayed to talk with us long after the performance was over.

The holy city of Ujjain is home to 108 temples. Hindu temples, Muslim mosques, and Christian churches can be seen throughout the city, a common destination of spiritual pilgrimages.

In May 2016, a severe storm caused deaths during one of the largest religious festivals in the world. Kumbh Mela takes place in Ujjain every twelve years and attracts as many as 70,000,000 pilgrims from all over India. A large tent collapsed killing many. Hundreds of temporary structures collapsed burying dozens of devotees and injuring many. People panicked. Most were far from home and without food, water, and shelter. The Islamic mosques of Ujjain opened their doors to Hindus seeking shelter. This is India at its best.

The most famous Hindu temple in Ujjain is the Shree Mahakaleshwar Temple. Devotees of Shiva come to visit this temple from all over India. Cameras, mobile phones, and shoes are forbidden in the temple complex. Some temples allow visitors to take photos, and others do not. It's a shame, because my friends would appreciate them. I understand why they disallow photography; it just saddens me when they do.

What is even tougher for me is going shoe-less — that arch issue again. I deal with it to view the inside of a temple respectfully but, while my heart is Indian, my feet are the feet of a four-year-old girl, only much bigger, American size 12, European size 46. The only times I ever remove my shoes is when I take a bath or a shower and when I go to bed at night. This makes for a pair of tender feet.

When a temple supplies a cloth bag for shoes, three or four pairs of shoes will fit in one bag. My huge sneakers always get a bag of their own. The only consolation is that I feel safe at temples where we are required to leave our shoes outside. Who is going to steal *mine*? Someone who wants to climb into one and paddle down a river? This made the Shree Mahakaleshwar Temple my least favorite of those I've visited in India. Miles of walking up and down ramps and stairs and broken cement floors and, even if you see something you like, just move along.

When we traveled anywhere, I would ride on the back of Nishchay's motor scooter. His friend, Ayush, would join us, and Judy would ride on the back of his scooter. Sometimes Arya would ride in front of Ayush. This is common in India. I've seen as many as five adults on one motorcycle! It's also common to carry enormous loads on a scooter or cycle.

Most motorcycles in India have small 100 cc to 150 cc engines. I have owned motorcycles with engines as large as 1400 cc, which would be much too cumbersome and not nearly nimble enough for Indian traffic. Larger engines are available in India, but are not popular. Most Indians want to squeeze as much functionality and petrol (gas) economy out of their transportation as possible.

Indians have a great word for creatively breaking the rules to accomplish a task. The word is "jugaad", pronounced jew-GAHD. A person who gets things done creatively against all odds, or by breaking rules, is called "jugaadu" (jew-GAH-doo). This applies to anyone riding the 110 cc motorbike with 200 kilos (440 pounds) of lumber strapped behind him.

Language misunderstandings can be comical. When I first began chatting with Nishchay online, he urged me to come to India during a Diwali celebration. He felt that, if I enjoyed Holi so much in 2015, I'd love Diwali even more. He warned me: *"Diwali can be dangerous because everyone throws crackers in the street."* Ritz Crackers? Saltine Crackers? I tried to imagine Indians tossing food into the streets. Wasteful, sure, but how would this be dangerous? Headline: *"MAN SLIPS ON A FRUIT BISCUIT DURING DIWALI AND BREAKS HIS NECK!"* When Nishchay described the *noise* of the crackers, I asked him, "Do you mean *fire*crackers?" In India, they're simply called "crackers".

On the night of Diwali, Akshay insisted that I light the family's first fireworks. I kicked off the evening's event by lighting a huge string of 2,000 firecrackers! Families throughout the neighborhood lit fireworks for many hours.

In some Indian states, Diwali lasts for five days; other states celebrate for as many as fifteen days. The lights symbolize destruction of all negative forces. Lights decorating homes serve as an invitation for the goddess, Lakshmi, to enter and bless the family with prosperity. "Deeps" or "handi lamps" (small clay oil lamps) are also lit throughout homes for this purpose. I felt honored that I was asked to launch and participate in such an important traditional celebration.

There is a wonderful saying in Hindi, "Atithi Devo Bhava", which means, "The guest is God." The Maheshwaris went one step further. They made us feel like FAMILY.

Diwali was a blast! Families lit fireworks and rockets and sparklers and spinners. There were "BOOMS" that shook the pavement. What fun!

Ujjain had another nice surprise for us. Nishita Singh, a beautiful and elegant young woman we met when we first arrived, surprised us with *rose-flavored milkshakes*. They are so good! I now buy rose syrup online for making milkshakes and rose-flavored lassis, thanks to Nishita's shared recipes.

I'd been away from home for about a month and realized I needed a haircut. Nishchay took me by motor scooter to see his barber. Patrons waiting their turn looked surprised and stared curiously at seeing a foreigner.

The owner of the barbershop decided to cut my hair himself. To say he was meticulous would be an understatement. I hope brain surgeons take their jobs this seriously! He took a break, halfway through the haircut, and we all had a cup of masala chai. After finishing my hair he massaged my scalp, then my face and neck, then my shoulders. The barber told Nishchay (in Hindi) that I could return anytime and that he would use his *electric* massager on me. As usual, Nishchay refused to let me pay for my haircut and massage, which totaled a whopping 50 rupees (75 cents USD).

Shopping in Ujjain's marketplace was fun. I bought Indian stickers to decorate a few of my drums, and a brass prayer bell to share the "fire alarm" story at home.

On a day that I took a walk by myself, I sat on a bench in a nearby park where two pre-teen boys noticed me and began talking excitedly in Hindi. I imagine that the conversation went like this:

Boy 1: "*You* talk with him!"

Boy 2: "*I'm* not gonna talk with him! *You* talk with him!"

Boy 1: "What would I even say? He probably speaks English or Italian or some other weird language!"

Boy 2: "How about if we just touch his feet? He's an old guy. He's like my grandfather's age. We could touch his feet!"

Boy 1: "Great idea! You go first!"

Boy 2: "*I'm* not going first!"

The two boys came into the park from the street taking the long way around to where I was sitting. Like a thief robbing a purse, the first boy reached down and touched my feet quickly. I said, "Happy Diwali!" He froze, made eye contact with me for the first time, and looking confused replied, "Happy Diwali".

The second boy was a bit more relaxed. The trail had been blazed. The foreigner hadn't killed his friend. He touched my feet, and we wished each other a Happy Diwali. The two boys then left the park to tell their friends. For fifteen minutes, curious heads popped up over the wall to check me out.

Nishchay had an idea. Since he was leaving on Sunday for Indore where he was catching a bus to Pune, and we were leaving on Monday for Indore to visit Deepika, Nishchay proposed that we go with him on Sunday and that he drop us at our friend's home. I wrote to Deepika about the plan and she loved it.

Deepika Verma is the only one of my Indian sons and daughters who I've known for more than five years. We met online when she was a college student and got to know each other well enough that she shared personal problems and concerns with me. During one of our conversations she called me her "Angel Paa". I had not considered myself a father figure to anyone on the other side of the world. Deepika started it. I had made *that* big a difference in a young person's life by opening my heart.

Our itinerary for this trip to India was nearly firmed up when I reached Deepika after having lost touch for several years. We borrowed a few days from other agendas to travel to Indore. Nishchay's suggestion would add a half day to that visit. I was excited.

Nishchay gave us a gift from his family--a piece of art depicting three Ganeshas, two playing drums and one playing harmonium. This is a perfect reminder of the three of us making music together in Ujjain. It was in Ujjain that I pointed out to Judy how our stay with each family was "completely different and completely awesome". This sentiment would continue to hold true for the visits to come.

When we woke the next morning, I told Judy how proud and happy I am that she is my wife. Since our arrival in India, she had endured inconveniences without complaint. She had no relationship with any of the young people or their families who had hosted us, and yet she had earned everyone's affection, returning it wholeheartedly. She had earned the names, "Judy Maam", "Chaachi", and "mom". I feel lucky that she is my wife and it seemed a good time to tell her.

On Sunday, before the driver arrived to take us to Indore, Arya sat beside Nishchay sobbing, sad that her big brother was leaving again for his job in Pune. Judy and Susmita shared a teary goodbye, then Susmita said, "I feel bad. I'm going to miss you." I hugged each family member. I was going to miss them deeply.

Our driver showed up thirty minutes late. He was hired to bring Nishchay to the bus terminal and then bring Judy and me to Deepika's house. Once on the road, we learned that the driver wasn't at all familiar with Indore. We altered the plan: we would all get off at the bus station (if the driver could find it), and ask Deepika's family to pick us up there.

During the hour-long ride from Ujjain to Indore, Nishchay rested his head on Judy's shoulder. I thought how difficult it must be for him to spend months away from home, then return to Diwali and family for a short time, and now take a fourteen-hour bus ride and return to Pune for several more months. Nishchay is so focused and diligent, it's easy to forget he's only nineteen years old.

Once we reached Indore, the driver must have asked six times for directions to the bus station. One man was generous enough to ride with us and direct the driver. We should have been quite early for Nishchay's bus. Instead, we were in danger of being late. If Nishchay missed this bus, he would have to take another the following day and miss a day's work at a new job. We were all on edge. Judy suggested that, if Nishchay missed his bus, we could ask Deepika if he could stay at her house overnight.

When we finally reached the bus station, Nishchay inquired about his bus at the ticket office and was told that it hadn't arrived yet. Not trusting this information, he crossed the street to where several buses were parked and learned that his bus to Pune *was* there and preparing to leave. We said a rushed goodbye. Nishchay ran across the street toward the bus but then crossed back toward us again. We were confused. He had his tickets. The bus was about to leave. Why was he running back this way? Did he forget something?

Nishchay hurriedly touched my feet and then Judy's feet before running back to the bus.

I wiped my eyes.

INDORE

After waiting for ten minutes or so, Judy said, "Someone is waving from that car."

It was Deepika. Her brother Kunal whom I recognized from Facebook, was driving. I gave Deepika a very long-overdue hug, Kunal got our luggage into the car, and off we went.

Deepika Verma is one of the most openhearted and loving individuals I know. She is shy, friendly, warm, and kind. She is very spiritual and loves animals. Every time I looked at Deepika, I couldn't believe we were in the same room together after all these years. She was between jobs which, from a financial standpoint, was a problem; however, she was grateful to be free to spend time with us. That is my beautiful, loving Deepika.

When we got to the house we were not allowed to lift a single bag. We met their mother, Lata, and their father, Ramesh, who had transformed the air-conditioned parlor into our bedroom. We talked for awhile and, like many parents, Deepika's mother and father seemed to understand more English than they spoke. It was clear that these were very nice people.

Deepika set up a long coffee table in our room where we ate a delicious dinner. There was a dining room table in the next room, but Lata thought we'd be more comfortable in our room. It took a day to convince her that we're more comfortable eating at a dining room table.

This happened often during our visits. Most westerners are accustomed to sitting down and eating together. For us, mealtime is as much a social experience as a biological need. Some host families watched while we ate, some left us alone to eat, and some eventually joined us. It wasn't a big deal, but it served as a small reminder of our cultural differences.

Deepika told us about a recent experience. She went to a popular and famous ashram east of Delhi, where she listened to and was moved by the wisdom and demeanor of the guru there. She found the meditation techniques to be beneficial. By the end of the month, she was so moved and impressed that she quit her job and accepted a full-time position working for the ashram.

Once she was employed there, she was in a better position to speak with the guru. When she asked him for clarification on some of his *teachings*, she was accused of being "negative" and told to follow his words without question. When a woman's clothing had been ruined by mold in her ashram quarters, she asked if the ashram would help pay to have them laundered. The guru maintained that the woman was demonstrating "negativity", which he could not tolerate. The ashram took no financial responsibility for the mold damage.

It occurred to Deepika that this was little more than a lucrative business. Foreigners were charged a considerable amount of money (much more than Indians) to cook their own food and to clean up after themselves for the privilege of listening to the guru's well-rehearsed patter.

So she quit. Sometimes we get to see the "man behind the curtain" to use a reference from the Wizard of Oz.

I told her, "There is no wisdom without kindness."

That evening, two pre-teen sisters who are students of Deepika, came to the house for a visit. The older sister had written a song and came to sing it to me.

"Rick Cormier, Rick Cormier; You are so sweet, you are so sweet; Our national crop is wheat..."

She had me at, "You are so sweet".

Later that evening, two boys joined the two girls and we talked about all sorts of things. They said that they would love to see what American money looks like and asked if I had any to show them. One of the boys proudly announced that he would prefer to see *British* money. I knew I had both American and British coins in my carry-on bag, so after successfully fishing through the bag, I handed each of the first three kids a quarter, a dime, and a nickel for them to keep. I then gave the fourth kid a British one pound coin. I didn't mention that the British pound was worth many times more than the US coins.

The next day, The Verma family planned a road trip to Maheshwar. Deepika's dad wanted us to see rural India, so we took the long way through the winding roads of rural India. I was so happy that we did!

During the drive we saw wide open vistas, distant mountain views, and strange but beautiful trees and wildflowers. We saw countless straw houses and farmers working without farm equipment. People picked cotton in fields and stuffed it into large cloth bags that hung from their shoulders. I waved to some kids who excitedly waved back. This was far from the typical tourist experience, but given a choice of seeing this or the Taj Mahal, I'd choose this every time. These were people surviving, raising children, growing crops, and hoping that their kids would somehow have an easier life.

Deepika's dad is the chief engineer for the water treatment facilities that supplies the city of Indore with clean water. We stopped and toured several of the water treatment facilities and had tea and cookies at a few government rest stops along the way. At one of these stops, Deepika showed me an enormous old banyan tree that she loved as a young girl. I took pictures of her posing in front of her tree. We later stopped for lunch at one of the government houses.

Ramesh is "non-veg", so we followed his lead and ordered the curried fish. Ramesh later received an urgent call — he was needed at one of the water treatment facilities — so he had to leave. Kunal drove us to the palace at Maheshwar. After hours of driving we reached our destination to happily discover that it was well worth the trip.

First, a bit of history: Maharani Ahilyadevi Holkar (later to be fondly called "Ahilyabai") was born in 1725 of a non-royal lineage. Women did not attend school in those days, but her father taught her to read and write. She was married to Maharaja Khanderao Holkar, in 1733 at the age of eight.

To make a long story short, war was a popular pastime in those pre-cricket days. Ahilyabai's husband died in battle and then her father-in-law was killed. Her son became the ruler of Malwa, which included a portion of the modern states of Madhya Pradesh and Rajasthan. Months later, he died. In 1767, at the age of 42, Ahilyabai became the Queen and ruler of Malwa. One year into her rule, when invaders attacked, she successfully led her armies into battle; she herself slaying enemies using swords, bows, and arrows.

Though her palace was in Maheshwar, 95 km (60 miles) away, she was responsible for transforming Indore from a small village to a prosperous major city. She built dozens of temples, ghats (stairways that lead to a body of water), wells, and rest-houses from the Himalayas to pilgrimage centers in South India. Merchants and farmers thrived under her rule, as she believed she had no right to their profits and refused to tax them. She held public audiences daily so that her subjects could voice their complaints and concerns. Maheshwar became a center of literary, musical, artistic, and industrial enterprise. During her thirty-year reign, Malwa enjoyed unprecedented peace and prosperity.

I wish I had known all of this when I first saw Ahilyabai's statue in her gardens. I knew nothing of her history.

I took a few photos in the palace gardens. Then we removed our shoes (sigh) and walked the perimeter of an area dedicated to Ahilyabai. We were walking along a lengthy ghat that leads to the Narmada River when — I nearly froze.

The architecture became incredible. I couldn't believe my eyes! We were now high at the top of a hill looking down on a vista of stunningly beautiful temples with the wide Narmada River flowing behind them. My camera and I got really busy. I couldn't possibly put into words the beauty of this view. (I encourage readers to take time on the internet to view the photos of Ahilya Fort.)

After touring the castle, temples, ghat, vendors, and the boats moored along the water's edge, Deepika suggested we take a boat ride. Kunal bought our tickets, and we enjoyed a beautiful trip on the Narmada River while sunset turned to night.

While leaving the palace and heading to our car, we walked past a strange-looking building with rows of narrow cut-outs no bigger than four or five feet wide; each was covered with a cloth curtain. When I asked about them, Deepika explained, to my surprise, that they are "apartments" for the homeless as a place to sleep and as refuge from the weather. As it turns out, Queen Ahilyabai also cared for the poor and the homeless during her reign. She was the sort of leader any country would benefit from — then and now.

Deepika wouldn't let us pay for the boat tour. In fact, she wouldn't let us pay for anything. Whenever she saw me admiring something she would say, "Do you like that, Paa? Can I buy that for you, Paa?" She was unemployed and yet insisted on paying our way. Deepika wouldn't even let me move a chair three feet! "Let me move that for you, Paa." There were times when I wanted to tell her, "*You're* the 'angel', not me."

Even More Interesting Facts and Observations:

1. Most of the cars we saw in India were white. This makes sense when you consider how much sunlight beats down on cars on India.

2. Most (maybe all?) cars in India are manual shift. This makes sense when you consider the driving skill required in Indian traffic.

3. India has also learned one of the worst sides of Western civilization — our commercial marketing side. Don't be surprised to find "Om Tires," "Laxmi's Turmeric," "Namaste Pizza Crust Mix," "Sita's Savory Sauce," or "Krishna's Crispy Ladoos" the next time you shop.

4. Indian showers: I don't mean rain or monsoons. I mean taking a shower in India. Not as a tourist staying in an Americanized hotel, but as an American member of an Indian family.

    There is a shower head but, in all but one of our experiences, no hot water comes out of it. There is, however, a hot water faucet below on the wall. When Judy first spotted the big plastic buckets in the bathroom, she assumed that they were left behind after a cleaning.

    Wrong.

    After our first few family visits, Judy figured out that a big bucket is filled with hot water, which is then poured over the body with the small, handheld, plastic pitcher that accompanied each big bucket. Judy pointed out that this was an excellent way to conserve water!

5. Some Indian homes and restaurants have western toilets, but some Indians don't fully understand that westerners from North America clean ourselves with toilet paper instead of water.

   I know, I know. The Indian way is better. But we've been wiping our bums with paper since we were little. A western toilet without toilet paper is a real predicament for us. The hose and sprayer next to the toilet seem as helpful to us as a hammer and a plate of sweets. Thankfully, we brought small rolls of camping toilet paper with us for situations such as this.

6. Most of our host-family moms dialed back the spiciness of their food when we first arrived. It's understandable. We're American. Most Americans aren't even adventurous enough to use ground black pepper! It's important to understand that many American's families were originally from countries like England, France, Poland, Ireland, Germany, etc. where spices are seldom used.

   Well, I'm Acadian by heritage. My Louisiana cousins are called Cajuns and are known for their spicy food and hot sauce. When I'm in a Thai restaurant and am asked to choose "How spicy from zero to five?", I've been known to answer "ten". I'm lucky if what I get is even a three.

When we first told Deepika that we would like to shop at the marketplace, she was very protective of us. Her initial concerns were that we might become exhausted from all of the walking or be uncomfortable with the crowds. We insisted that neither walking nor bazaar crowds bothered us in the least. Still, when we reached the marketplace and began to browse, Deepika apologized for the sheer number of people. I reassured her that we love people and that crowds don't bother us.

We visited several shops that sold brass items. Nishchay had already convinced me that Saraswati is my personal guiding Hindu goddess. For a Christian to understand Hindu gods and goddesses, it is best to think of them as you would saints. Hindus are free to have differing beliefs about God. Like Buddhists and Unitarians, they respect the paths of others, but most Hindus also have a favorite deity or deities, as each is thought to symbolize a particular knowledge, energy, or power.

Saraswati is depicted sitting on a lotus, playing a large stringed instrument called a vina, which looks like a sitar. In her four arms she also holds a book and a pen. She is the goddess of wisdom, knowledge, music, and the arts. One source I found interpreted her name to mean "one who leads to the essence of self-knowledge". That sounds like psychotherapy to me. I could do worse than to be "blessed by Saraswati".

When I spotted a beautifully-detailed, four-inch brass statue of Saraswati, I waited for Deepika to be distracted with Judy before making a deal. The vendor wanted 1000 rupees for the statue, but I held firm at 500 rupees ($7.50 in USD). He weighed the brass on a scale, decided he was still making a profit, and sold it to me for 500 rupees.

It was time to stock up on my home supply of cardamom. While browsing at the marketplace, I told Deepika I needed to find the spice merchants. She got directions and led us through the crowded streets past fruit and vegetable vendors and jewelry merchants until we reached the spice vendors.

I knew that two things were true: 1) I needed to buy enough cardamom to last me another year or so and, 2) My sweet and loving Deepika would try to pay for it. Once we determined which vendors sold ground cardamom, I waited until she was again busy with Judy and paid for my own cardamom. Unfortunately, I needed more than the first vendor had, which required me to sneak a purchase from *a second* vendor. In the end, I got my supply of cardamom and I managed to pay for it myself.

When we finally reached home, it was Deepika who was exhausted.

I must add that Deepika wins the "Best Music Award". The music she played on the car stereo was the only music we would search for upon returning home. My personal favorite is sitar backed by bass guitar and modern drumming. Deepika is one of those who believes that my contemporary drumming style would attract young Indians to kirtan. I am told by young Indian friends that the more traditional kirtan music attracts only their grandparents.

The music Deepika played was always backed by drumming that grooved with feeling and made one's body want to move. That left room for the rest of the music to speak to the mind and spirit. She called it, "good yoga music".

The evening before our departure, being aware of my struggle with arthritic knees, Deepika had me videotape her doing yoga exercises that she felt could help me. She also gave me a gift of a book called, "Intelligence Without Thought" by Dada Gavind.

When I think of Nandita from Jaipur, I recall her keen intellect and deep passion for women's social issues. When I think of Archana from Kota, I'm reminded of her commitment as a wife and mother, along with the utter joy she emanates. Nishchay from Ujjain exudes talent, focus, and determination. Deepika embodies the loving heart. She is bright, talented, and beautiful — but it's her heart that runs the show.

When I look objectively at the other young people I consider daughters and sons of my heart, including Piyush, Darsika, Saila, Nipanjana, Javeria, Trupti, Rachna, Riya, Shivanshi, Pradeep, Harsh, Prachi, Madhu, and Suvarna, I see how different from one another they are — and how completely awesome.

When it was time for me and Judy to leave Indore and fly to Nagpur, Deepika's father took the day off from work, drove many miles home, and joined Deepika and Kunal to see us off at the airport.

As enjoyable as these visits were, the goodbyes were getting harder each time. It felt as though my heart would burst if I said goodbye to another of these beautiful souls.

How can I explain the feeling of knowing someone so well online, sharing their joys and disappointments, becoming so close that you feel that they are already a part of your family, regularly sending virtual smiles, hearts, and hugs? Suddenly we meet and that long-awaited hug becomes real. We've never met before, and yet we know each other so well. We finally get to spend time together and enjoy each other's company for a matter of days.

Until the time comes to say goodbye.

Goodbyes are hard and this one was no exception. Most airports in India don't allow non-passengers to enter the airport, so we had to say our goodbyes on the street in front of the airport entrance.

Saying goodbye to this young woman who half a decade ago declared me her "Angel Paa" was difficult.

Even now, I'm getting choked up just writing about it.

AMRAVATI

Indigo Airlines charged us *4500 rupees* (about $70.00 USD) for exceeding the checked baggage allowance (though we still would have been well within the limits for US or international travel). This was more than the cost of each of our tickets! We could have bought a seat for a third person, handed him a piece of our luggage, and saved money!

Nagpur, where we landed, is the third largest city in the Indian state of Maharashtra after Mumbai and Pune. It's known as the "Orange City," not because it looks orange in an aerial view the way Jaipur looks pink and Bundi looks blue but because it's a major trade center of oranges cultivated in that region.

Neha Photani, who we were going to Amravati to visit, is a Sindhi. That meant nothing to me when we first met online so let me provide a brief explanation:

When Pakistan broke from India in 1947 to create a separate Muslim country, Sindh was one of the original Indian states that found itself in the middle of the new "Pakistan". This politically-motivated partitioning was poorly planned and turned extremely violent, dividing Hindus and Muslims. As Hindus left their homes in the newly-formed Pakistan, and Muslims left their homes in what remained of India, as many as two million people were killed and fourteen million displaced. Many of the Hindus and Sikhs in Sindh abandoned their homes and left Pakistan for modern-day India, where the majority of the people were Hindu.

This turned out to be a wise decision, as the Hindus are now a minority in Pakistan and often treated accordingly.

That's the history. My reality is that I have never felt so welcomed — so *held* — as I have by the Sindhi community. More on that to come.

In person, Neha struck me as a smart, beautiful, dignified, quiet young woman who is very observant and sensitive to people's needs and feelings. Online, she and I have been particularly close. We have discussed everything under the sun. Religion, politics, relationships, culture, personal successes and challenges — no subject is off-limits. If I have a potentially embarrassing question to ask about Indian culture, I ask Neha. When she has a question and doesn't want to be made to feel silly for asking, she asks me. The only time we disagreed vehemently, we shelved the argument as unimportant. She is one of very few I call "Betiya", an affectionate Hindi term for "daughter", and she calls me "Dad". Several times during our visit we looked at one another and expressed disbelief that we were finally meeting face-to-face.

Neha and her cousin "Appy" came to the Nagpur airport to meet Judy and me. We shared a heartfelt hug. She had hired an Uber cab to take us to her aunt's house. Neha's home is in Amravati, but she works in Nagpur. During the week, she lives at her Aunt Sarita's house in Nagpur and travels the three hours to Amravati most weekends. Tonight, we would be staying at her aunt's house before heading to Amravati the next day.

On arrival at Sarita's home we met her and many of Neha's cousins and their children. Her aunt and some cousins each have apartments upstairs from a Ganesha temple. Sindhis tend to live in close-knit communities, so there are lots of Sindhis in this neighborhood.

Aunt Sarita was well-prepared for our arrival with a wonderful dinner feast. After dinner, Neha asked if we would like to go for a walk. We walked around the neighborhood for about an hour, stopping for ice cream before heading back. We sat and talked more with everyone before heading to bed. Sleeping was a challenge. The bed was designed for much shorter people. It was okay. Nothing could ruin this experience.

The next day we met Neha's brother Nishant ("Nishu") and her father Dilipkumar. Nishu drove us to Neha's work where we were introduced to her manager and coworkers. She had asked her manager, Ranjit Singh, CEO and Managing Director of Syslogyx, for the week off from work. This was quite a request considering the time she would be taking in early December for her brother's wedding, followed by her cousin Madhu's wedding several days later. She explained that her "American dad" was coming to visit, and wanted to spend as much time with us as possible. Neha was impressed with her manager's understanding, and was grateful for the time off.

We were led to a conference room where we met Mr. Singh. I thanked him for having given Neha the time off, and he spoke very eloquently about how a manager must consider the lives of his employees if he is going to expect their loyalty and best efforts.

I was impressed. I would have considered coming out of retirement and working for him myself but the commute would have killed me.

We talked about India and American politics and our plans for the week. He suggested that we visit Deekshabhoomi, the major pilgrimage center of Buddhism in India. After more than a half hour of conversation, he invited us to the central office area to meet his staff. Neha introduced us to her coworkers, then she announced that I would explain how we knew one another. Neha's coworkers got the short, oral version of this book: From the airport to the Bengali wedding to Quora to "Baapu". Now some of *them* are my Facebook friends!

Judy and Neha thought I did fine, but I'm never prepared to make speeches. When I was a young man, I avoided public speaking the way most people avoid big, hairy spiders. When I was eighteen, I read where Ralph Waldo Emerson said, "Always do what you are afraid to do". He ruined my life. He shook me out of my comfort zone forever with that one line.

Afterward, Nishu drove us to Deekshabhoomi where millions of pilgrims visit every year. Its stupa (the main building) is circular, made of granite, marble, and local sandstone, and spreads across 4000 square feet. Five thousand monks can stay in each of its two stories. In front of the stupa is a Bodhi Tree, a sacred fig tree. It was planted from three branches of the original Bodhi Tree in Sri Lanka under which Gautama Buddha himself became enlightened.

From Deekshabhoomi, we drove to a beautiful area by a lake where young lovers go to be together. The walkway is decorated with beautifully-patterned white mosaic tiles. As anticipated, there were couples everywhere holding each other, hugging, and kissing while their parents thought they were doing something innocent and harmless like taking dance lessons at "Brahma's House of Bhangra".

Neha asked if I preferred to leave for Amravati that night or wait until the following day. Remembering the size of the bed at Aunt Sarita's house, I opted for leaving that night if her brother, Nishu, was agreeable to the three-hour drive.

Nishu is pretty incredible. Despite running three clothing stores, he graciously took time from his work to drive us around that week, with occasional help from cousins Aakask ("Guddu") and Prachant ('Mickey'). Nishu married in early December, a month after our departure from India. Dilipkumar had generously offered to put us up in a hotel if we could return to Amravati for the wedding but, sadly, the cost of roundtrip airfare to India made it impossible.

On the way to Amravati, we stopped at a vegetarian restaurant. I had been warned that Ujjain and Amravati probably would not have non-veg restaurants. At Indian restaurants in the United States, Chicken Makhani is one of my favorite dishes, so I ordered Dal Makhani. It consists of several types of lentils in a spicy sauce and is served on rice or roti. It is amazing! I now make it at home.

It was late by the time we reached the house in Amravati. As always, no one let us move our luggage, which appeared in our room as magically as it got packed into the car. We met Neha's mom, Hema, as well as several cousins.

Neha's cousin Madhu is a charming young woman and one of my Indian Facebook friends who calls me "Dad". She once made me an online collage of photos that said, "*If I know what love is . . . It's because of you.*" In the center of the collage is a photo of Judy and me surrounded by pictures of Madhu, Neha, and our son, Mike. Accompanying the collage was the message, "Your three beautiful and intelligent children". Madhu isn't as fluent in English as her cousin Neha, so our online conversations are more limited, but I know her heart. It was great to meet her in person.

Madhu cooked us a scrumptious breakfast one morning and a dinner of Palak Puri and Veg Biryani one night. Her new husband must be eating very well!

The hour was late, so we went to bed. Neha's parents had given up their bedroom for us. It included a huge, comfortable bed, air conditioning, and an attached bathroom with a western-style toilet — and toilet paper! Okay. So, I get excited about small blessings.

Our first morning in Amravati was memorable. Hema made coffee for Judy and masala chai for me. She also made lots of breakfast foods. I tried explaining that only Judy eats breakfast and that my first meal of the day is lunch. Hema has a funny routine. If you refuse food, she will suggest, "Half?" If you continue to refuse, she asks, "One quarter?" My resolve only faltered a few times during our stay.

The delicacies that came out of Hema's kitchen during our stay included Sambhar Wada, Tamatar Chatni, Moong Paratha, Bhindi Aalu, Dhaniya Chatni, Palak Puri, Sindhi Dhoda, Sindhi Koki, Pulao, Samosa, Dhokla, Dahi Bada, Geela Bada, Sabudana Chap, Sindhi Moong Mogar, Katori Chat, and Poha.

More than a dozen neighborhood kids, some related and some not, came to meet us. Neha had warned me that many people in Amravati had seen westerners only in the movies and on television. She hoped that we wouldn't be uncomfortable when people stared at us. I assured her that both of us understood any staring was out of curiosity, not animosity.

The neighborhood kids were charming, and fascinated with us. They would coach one another on what questions to ask us, such as: "What's your favorite color?" and "What's your favorite song?" Some spoke English quite well when you consider that they would likely have learned to speak Sindhi, Marathi (the official language of the state of Maharashtra), and Hindi before learning English. I'm Acadian, and I never managed to learn French! One neighborhood girl wrote "*Welcome Foreners!*" in chalk on a wall outside.

That morning, there was a steady stream of relatives and neighbors coming to the house to meet us. From time to time some of the neighborhood kids would peek into the open door to smile and wave at us. Dilipkumar teaches at a local school but also teaches each morning privately out of his home. A bunch of young teens began arriving, peeking into the parlor at us as they passed the open door. Neha said they wanted to meet us, so we stepped into the classroom.

It was soon apparent that they, too, expected a little speech in the way of introduction. I got through it. Every subsequent day, the girls would peek into the parlor and smile on their way to their classroom. Not the boys, of course. Teenage boys have to maintain that cool, detached image, even on *that* side of the world.

At one point, when Neha and I were alone in the front room together, I looked at her and said, "If I had a biological daughter, I would want her to be *you*." For a long time, she and I had ended our online conversations with the words, "I love you". I guess I wanted her to know that I was that guy and that I felt the same, if not more so, after having met her face-to-face.

At the end of our first full day in Amravati, Nishu returned us home at about or seven or eight o'clock. There were ten or twelve kids in front of Neha's house excitedly shouting something in their native language. It turned out they were saying, "They're here! They're here!" The kids crowded around us with huge smiles, giving hugs and handshakes. Judy took a picture of me with these kids before we went into the house.

During our time at Neha's, kids would peek their heads into the open door smiling and waving and sometimes they'd come into the house to talk with us. Neha's dad became concerned that the constant flow of local kids might be annoying us. I assured everyone that we weren't in the least bit annoyed.

A week earlier, when Nishchay was leaving his family home to return to Pune, his sister Arya reacted sad and teary. Nishchay looked at me with emotion and concern, not quite knowing what to do or say. I told him, "Be proud when someone feels this strongly about you. Not everyone will. Never take for granted anyone who considers you that important".

This was my attitude in Amravati. Judy and I would help form these kids' impressions of foreigners, as well as their self-esteem. How we reacted to them mattered. Whether we responded with an open or closed heart mattered. If they wanted to pop their heads in the door to say "Hi" every ten minutes, I would smile, wave, and say "Hi" back every ten minutes. When people practically lined up to take a selfie with us, no problem. I may never be that important to anyone again. I'm not annoyed. I take my own advice: Take no one for granted who considers you important.

Judy wanted to buy some more kurtis, so we went to Nishu's clothing store. Judy found a few kurtis off the rack and ordered a few outfits custom-made from fabrics she chose. While we were upstairs looking at cloth patterns, Nishu insisted we sit in the "owner's chairs". Neha wouldn't let Judy pay for a single outfit.

While Judy was choosing designs and being measured for her custom outfits, I waited in a part of the store that was managed by

Neha's cousin, Aakash. Again, I was invited to sit in the "owner's chair". (I later learned that several customers asked if the store was owned by Westerners.) For me, the funniest part was that many of the women who came into the store to buy kurtis and other apparel asked to take selfies with me. I always agreed, reminding myself that this beautiful city, particularly famous for women's clothing, is not one frequented by foreign tourists.

One Last Big Bunch of Interesting Facts and Observations:

1. Selfies. Indians with mobile phones have become obsessed with taking selfies since our visit here two years ago. Without exaggeration, my guess is we were asked to pose for more than 500 selfies during the last three weeks we were here--in stores, on the street, in parks, in homes, and even in temples we visited.

   One woman tried taking a selfie with Judy without her knowledge. She walked alongside and a bit ahead of Judy lining up the picture to include them both, hoping to go unnoticed. Judy did notice and good-naturedly rested her chin on the woman's shoulder from behind, smiled, and said "Hello!" She then agreed to pose voluntarily with the amused and embarrassed woman.

2. Group selfies are common. The funny part is that people wouldn't take just one photo. They would all switch places so that everyone had a turn standing next to us. Taking a selfie with a family could involve four to six poses.

   One of my favorite observations about selfie-takers is that they all seem to have what I call a "selfie face". It looks nothing like the face with which they approach the world. It looks nothing like the face with which they converse. It is a well-practiced expression they reserve for selfies. It might be a friendly face or a sexy face.

One young woman's selfie face was a look of total surprise in each photo, as though someone took the shot without her knowledge!

3. Mothers stay at home. We met some pretty awesome moms during this trip — women who we really enjoyed spending time with. But when it came time to go anywhere, whether it was a trip to a park, a store, a restaurant, a temple, or just a simple walk around the neighborhood, moms stayed home.

    I'm sure this is a carryover of the traditional values of their generation. Moms are responsible for the cleaning, laundry, and cooking. I'm not suggesting they are prisoners of their homes. In fact, many of them work or take classes, and I'm sure that they shop for the family groceries. They are valued family members who we only saw at home.

4. No one wears seat belts! I'll be the first to admit that I only began wearing one ten years ago when our local law enforcement attached a hefty fine for not doing so. Apparently, seat belts are required by law in India but, outside of major cities like Delhi, Mumbai, and Bangalore, that law is pretty much ignored.

    This is even more ironic when you consider the *traffic* in India! I talked with Piyush about this recently. He laughed and reminded me that Indians love breaking the law (a sentiment I heard from several people during this visit). Piyush said that drivers use seatbelts more consistently in major cities like Delhi and Mumbai because there are more police enforcing the law. Piyush also said that there are t-shirts with an image of a seat belt diagonally across the shirt to fool police!

Once Judy was finished buying and ordering kurtis, Neha announced that it was time to find some kurtas for me. I explained to her that the street merchants did not sell kurtas that fit me. She decided we should concentrate our efforts on the men's clothing shops. The first clothing shop we tried had a few kurtas that fit, but were very plain. As I mentioned earlier, in the United States my size is Extra Large (XL). In India, the size that fits me is 4XL (XXXXL)! This is quite deflating for the guy who eats less than the Maheshwari family parrot. We had better luck at the next clothing store where, after climbing several narrow flights of stairs, the salesman showed us dozens of beautiful kurtas.

Shopping in Indian clothing stores can be overwhelming. Several store clerks attend to a customer at once. Once you tell them what you want, they begin to pull out and present multiple boxes of clothing. There must have been at least twenty boxes on the counter, with the clerk opening the boxes faster than I could look at them. When there was nothing that I liked, no problem, another twenty boxes were pulled out.

I narrowed the selection to three beautiful kurtas. Before this trip, I had sold some of my native flutes to have spending money in India. I spent some of it on the Rajasthani kurtas made for me by Nandita's aunt. I was now prepared to spend more, though there would be no 'family discount' here. Neha would not let me pay. Even after an attempted negotiation that she pay for one and I pay for two, she insisted that they were a gift. All she asked in return is that I wear them when I drum in kirtans with Santa Fe's "Bhakti Boogie Kirtan Band," and that I send her pictures of me in each outfit, which I did. The three kurtas needed alterations for length so a salesmen measured me before we headed for home.

Judy and I both developed a cough. Judy was sure that she was getting over a cold while I was sure that mine was a result of nearly six weeks of humidity. My lungs were used to humidity when we lived in the northeastern U.S. but, after four years in the southwest, humidity was less-easily tolerated. Now, humidity felt like breathing hot gravy. I guessed that this annoying cough would stop a few days after returning home, and it did.

Neha did not dismiss our coughs that easily.

Indians are very much into natural cures and turmeric has been valued for its medicinal properties for thousands of years. Today, Western medical science is confirming many of turmeric's virtues. Neha asked her mother to make turmeric milk for Judy and me. I love the taste of hot turmeric milk as much as I do hot chocolate. It is simply hot milk with about a half teaspoon of turmeric, sweetened to taste. Judy had never tasted it, and she loved it! Hema made us turmeric milk each night before bed, which Judy considered a very caring, comforting remedy. It didn't fix my cough, but it tasted great. Two days after we returned home our coughs were gone. Judy still makes herself a glass of hot turmeric milk each night.

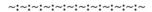

Neha's cousin, Swati, cooked us a delicious dinner of Sambar Vada and Methi Pulao one evening. Meeting Swati was a memorable experience. I had seen her in so many of Neha's online photos that, when I first met her, it was as though I knew her already. I gave her a pair of the earrings that I made.

One morning we went to visit more of Neha's relatives. We met Vaishali Chanchlani, who suggested we visit the local school that she and Neha had attended. Neha explained how the Holy Cross English High School is the best academic school in Amravati and difficult to get into. It is a girl's school run by Catholic nuns who also run an orphanage on the school grounds.

When we reached the school a bunch of teens were rehearsing a dance in the gym. A school guard kept us from going inside, since the entrance was too close to the rehearsal area. Vaishali took us to another building and rang the doorbell. (I admitted that, in my youth, I would ring convent doorbells and then ran away, until the one time I slipped on wet leaves chipping my front tooth, which ended a satisfying prank doorbell-ringing career.)

But I digress . . .

A nun, Sister Pushpa, greeted us at the door. Vaishali explained that she and Neha both graduated from the school and had come for a visit. Sister Pushpa led us inside to a sitting room. She explained that she is from Kerala in southern India and talked about the school and the programs offered there. She took us to the building where the teen girls were rehearsing their dance. This time we got in.

Sister Pushpa then brought us to the orphanage, which was a heart-wrenching experience. Imagine a room of infants ranging in age from several days to several months, each in a small crib. Sister Pushpa explained that these are babies of unwed mothers, couples who can't afford to feed a child, and of parents who don't want a girl.

This surprised me. I was aware that, many years ago, female babies were sometimes put to death, or put in the trash, or given up for adoption in India, but *today*? Sister Pushpa said that, while the situation has improved greatly, it still exists. Babies are still found in the trash in some places but, more often, the convent doorbell rings at two o'clock in the morning and the nuns find a baby outside the door.

The babies are well cared for. A woman remains in the nursery at all times feeding, changing, consoling, and monitoring the babies. A few others also work in the building. The younger babies are swaddled in small blankets; some being alert while others sleep. Neha cried as we went from baby to baby. I held it together and gave Neha an occasional hug. We smiled and talked with the babies and, in some cases, touched a tiny hand or face. Some of the babies were distressed by the interaction.

Some of them will be adopted. Those who aren't adopted attend school with the paying students. Sister Pushpa said that the orphanage students are fully integrated with and accepted by the other students. The paying students learn the importance of caring for others through their friendships with children who have been abandoned. For those who don't succeed in school, there is a program where they can learn a trade. We were told that some of the staff we met are not nuns, but abandoned children who graduated from the school and were hired as employees.

We then went outdoors where we met an older nun. She told us the story of a male child they raised who was lucky enough to be adopted and then raised in France. As he reached adulthood he became curious about his origins, but his adoptive mother discouraged his return to India, as she was afraid he would not want to remain with her. When his mother died, he flew to India to visit the orphanage, where he met and spoke with the nuns and stayed for several days. He spent much of his time with the babies, knowing that he was once one of them.

That story got to me. I told Neha that I was glad I was wearing sunglasses.

We next visited an area where the sisters care for adults who are developmentally handicapped. The program is part of "Mother Teresa's Missionaries of Charity". There were friendly faces and blank ones. One woman stepped up and sang an old Bollywood song. When we clapped for her, she launched into another song.

I came away amazed at the work these sisters are doing. They run an orphanage, a trade school, and a home for the developmentally-handicapped. They also run a grade school and a high school for 2,500 female students, both having high academic standards and results.

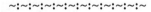

The Photani family wanted us to do a concert knowing that most of the local Sindhi community would want to attend, so we started making a plan. Judy had two of her flutes with her, but I wasn't able to bring a djembe drum to India. Vaishali helped by asking around about available drums. I was offered an electronic drum, which I refused, because electronic drums are in no way compatible with a wooden flute. Someone offered an "orchestral drum" (a tympani?) that I also refused for the same reason. I kept telling everyone not to worry, I could drum on a big plastic bucket! No one believed me and showed it with frowns each time I suggested it.

As it turned out, the local Sikh community was planning a big event at which a guru was going to speak. This gave Dilipkumar an idea. Why not ask to do a concert as part of the big event? Hundreds of community members would be there! We just needed to ask the permission of the committee which was scheduled to meet at ten o'clock that night. He was positive that they would agree.

In the meantime, we took tours of several beautiful temples. One particular Sikh temple had a wonderful kirtan band. Nishu talked with the leader of the band (probably mentioning that I drum for an American kirtan group) who made a point of introducing himself to me. The band was pretty awesome. I took some video footage of them playing and chanting.

After the Sikh temple, we met Dilipkumar at a shop where the family was choosing wedding invitations for Madhu's and Nishu's weddings.

Again, the issue was raised about what I could use for a drum the next evening. I told everyone not to worry. A big plastic bucket would be fine. More frowns. They just weren't buying this idea.

Judy said, "Grab that plastic stool over there and show them what you can do." I played my first-ever stool solo! Everyone was amazed and delighted. When I finished, I said, "...and plastic buckets have a much better sound than plastic stools!" Neha was so proud of me, she was beaming.

I was concerned about the committee meeting we were scheduled to attend at ten o'clock, because we were nowhere near that neighborhood. Neha wasn't a bit worried. She said that India's time zone is called "IST: India Standard Time," but that Indians typically define IST as "Indian Stretchable Time". She was right. The committee didn't meet until eleven o'clock that night.

When we arrived at the meeting, we were greeted by about fifteen men. Someone explained, in their native language, our proposal for joining their event. As the group discussed this, the word "drum" kept coming up. Morose faces and frowns resulted. I wanted to explain that the *flute* was the lead instrument, and that my drum was flute backup only.

Mahima and her mother, Lakshmi, sat beside me. Mahima is one of the little neighborhood girls who greeted us upon our arrival in Amravati. She is one of the girls who would come into the house regularly to say hi and try to make conversation in English. She has the best smile I've ever seen. Her whole face smiles, even her nose! It didn't feel to me like this meeting was going in our favor, but every time I looked at Mahima, she'd flash the smile that made me smile.

Finally, someone (in English) filled us in on the conversation. A documentary was being filmed of the following night's event, and they were *in favor* of having us play. They discussed how long we should play, and asked how long we *wanted* to play and whether I needed an equalizer for the sound system. They were sure they could borrow or rent a proper drum for me. This was followed by the shaking of hands, taking of selfies, and eating of snacks. One of the committee members approached me and said that a prayer meeting was held at 4:30 each morning and they would like for me to attend.

4:30 AM??

I told him it wouldn't be possible for me to be awake for *any* event at that hour. He said that the two-hour service would be in Hindi, but he was sure I'd understand what was being said by the hand gestures alone. I repeated that it was unlikely I would be there, especially if I were going to be drumming that evening.

Apparently, it is standard to make announcements at the end of the morning meeting and our performance *was not* mentioned. In fact, we didn't hear from any of the event coordinators the entire day. We guessed that my failure to appear at the 4:30 AM prayer service was a deal breaker. We were scratched from the program.

Dilipkumar was undaunted. He went up on the roof of his home and set up floodlights and arranged chairs and serving tables. He invited friends, relatives, and neighbors from the Sindhi community to the "Rooftop Concert" that would take place that evening.

Judy and I decided that we would improvise several flute and drum pieces and then play a drum duet together: in our case, a stool and bucket duet. Then Judy made a suggestion: "When we're finished, let's ask the audience to sing a song, and we'll drum along!" I had low expectations about the idea, but I agreed that we could try it.

There was a huge crowd on the roof. Adults, kids, and even a cricket team showed up! Long tables were set up with Chinese food for after the concert. If you need something done, call Dilip-kumar. I was amazed at what he managed to put together in one day. In fact, I later learned that he helped Neha plan the details of our entire week's visit.

We played our pieces to an appreciative and enthusiastic audi-ence. Judy then announced that we wanted *them* to sing some-thing, and *we* would drum along. So much for my low expecta-tions.

They chose a Sindhi song. Then another. They sang Bollywood songs they all knew, then a song in Hindi that had a verse about "a guy with a fat wife". A man in the audience was chosen who then took the hand of his overweight wife and together they jumped up and danced cheerfully. The next verse was about "a guy with a beautiful wife". They chose me. Judy and I got up and danced while everyone cheered loudly. They taught us to do a Sindhi dance. What fun! We had the most incredible time. We al-ready felt like part of the Photani family. That night we were made to feel a part of the entire Sindhi community. I'm teary as I write this.

Time to eat? Not quite yet. It was time for selfies! We spent the next half hour or more posing for selfies with people. We met and talked with such good-natured people in the process.

It was a joyous and moving night I'll never forget.

The next morning I decided to take a walk around Neha's neighborhood. It was a long walk and a nice time but, while I originally walked north of her house, I was pretty sure I wound up far south of her house. I reached an intersection and sensed that Neha's house was northeast of where I was standing. Should I go straight then right? Or should I turn right and then left? I must have had a confused look on my face because an unfamiliar old woman approached me. She didn't speak English, but made herself very clear by gesturing for me to go straight, then turn right.

What struck me funny was that she obviously knew in whose house the foreigners were staying. I clasped my hands and thanked her in Hindi and went on my way.

On the day before leaving Amravati, Neha and Nishu had a major three-hour road trip planned. Our ultimate destination was a park called Anand Sagar in the town of Shegaon. I had no idea what sort of park that was. Aakash drove. At the halfway point, we stopped at KT Food Products, a turmeric factory in Akola owned by Neha's Uncle Ramesh and managed by her cousin, Ashwin. There, we had a delicious breakfast provided by Neha's Aunt Rekha.

Again, everyone insisted that we sit in the "owner's chairs". I mentioned feeling weird about that to Neha the next day. She said that the eldest member of the family is the owner, even if he is not involved in the business. "You have a Sindhi daughter, and you're 64. That makes *you* the elder in our family. You belong in the owner's chair."

While I don't buy the logic, I deeply love the heart behind it.

I had no idea what to expect at Anand Sagar. A group of Neha's cousins met us at the factory to join us at the park. Our road trip turned into an automobile procession. We eventually began driving down many miles of dirt road. What could be here that was worth the three-hour drive?

Wow! The enormous figurines at the park entrance did a pretty good job of announcing that we had arrived at India's answer to Disneyland! The architecture is incredible. The park is full of hundreds of statues, amusement park rides, a lake, a train, temples, fountains, and the most massive children's playground I have ever seen. We took a train ride to see statues of animals that turned out to be no big deal, but the ride gave us a glimpse of the enormity of this park. It is one of those places where you can't possibly see everything in one day.

Tourists visit India and head straight to see the Taj Mahal where, today, you stand in line for Security to see the same image you see in every picture: a beautiful white building on a perpetually overcast day. You wait your turn to pose in front of the same rectangular pool of water, stand in line to enter the unlit building, walk around the sepulchre, and exit. One of the advantages of staying with families is getting to see and experience the things that *they* find enjoyable.

Did I mention that we posed for at least fifty more selfies while at the park? This was fun. We met lots more strangers. When Judy plopped her big, elegant hat on their little girl's head, adults understood that our commonalities as *people* far outweighed the differences in our cultures.

Neha's cousin, Karan, insisted that we go on a camel ride with him. Not a ride on a real camel, mind you, but a kiddie ride on a fake camel that bounced as it went around a track. We went. Many people took pictures of the big Anglo riding the silly camel, so I made faces like I was terrified. Karan then insisted I go on a ride that spun diagonally, high in the air. (At least this was a grown-up ride.) Judy wanted no part of it, so I went alone. When I got to the highest point in the ride, I spotted a sunset. I very carefully let go of the handrail, took out my camera trying to avoid rocking my seat too much, snapped a picture, and lived to tell the tale.

We looked like quite a mob as the ten of us walked down the streets of Anand Sagar heading toward the exit. I told Neha, Nishu, and their cousins, "If anyone asks, just say that you're all my children. Tell them that your *mother* is Indian." That got a good laugh.

Karan took over the driving for the trip home. We stopped at the turmeric factory again on our way back. Ashwin and his parents sent us home with two kilos of freshly ground turmeric (one for us and one for our son). We also received a kilo of besan (lentil flour), because of Judy's newfound love for the Indian dishes she planned to make with it.

On our last morning in Amravati, before heading back to Nagpur, Hema served Judy's usual two cups of coffee and my two cups of masala chai. We visited the school where Dilipkumar taught and met some of his fellow teachers. We said goodbye to the neighborhood kids and many of their moms. Hema expressed how sad she was that we were leaving. This led to another teary goodbye.

Nishu drove us back to Nagpur where we waited at Aunt Sarita's home until it was time to take our 3:00 AM flight.

Neha's cousins Nandini and Bharat had an eight-month-old son named Raunaq. He seemed to be a typical baby until he heard me drum on the table in front of me. To everyone's surprise, he began dancing! His parents had never seen him move this way before! Everyone laughed. Every time I drummed, Raunaq would gyrate his hips and thrust his little belly forward and backward. It was hysterical.

Little Raunaq, while playing on the floor, spotted a bug. He reached for the bug, grabbed it, and was about to eat it when someone snatched it away.

Someone said, "Here we are . . . a *vegetarian* family . . . who would have guessed that we were raising a non-veg child?!"

We headed for the airport where once again we had to say good-bye at the entrance. The airport employees and guards looked on with curiosity as we shared heartfelt hugs and tears. It was a long and emotional goodbye. I was sorry we would miss Nishu's and Madhus's weddings, but it was time for us to go. I looked forward to being home, and yet I hated leaving India. I looked forward to seeing my friends again, drumming in my drum circle, my blues band, my kirtan bands — and I hated leaving my sons and daughters and their families and the love they all so generously expressed.

They give me credit for being supportive, for being there when they need me, for being an "inspiration", and they may never fully understand how important each of them is to me.

I gave Neha one last hug. During the embrace, I said, "I love you so much!" It was true, and I wished I could express that sentiment to each of my Indian children. I knew only Neha and Deepika well enough to speak those words without the fear of being misunderstood.

It's no small thing when someone on the other side of the world considers you their "Baapu", or"Angel Paa", "Touji", "Baba" or "Dad". I take no one for granted who considers me important in their life. I feel blessed, and loved, and very lucky, not only because of our expanded family in India, but because of all of the people who are in my life by choice.

Since those early teen days in Catholic school, I've never considered myself very "religious". I dared to step back and see the world and all of its cultures and faiths. I saw religion and spiritu-ality as mankind's attempt to be better. But, whenever something awesome happened to me unexpectedly, even in my twenties, I called it a "report card from God". It was a message from God or the universe or life itself telling me that I was doing something right.

Interpret it as you will, but *all* of this happened because, in 2014, I reached out to a young woman behind me in line at an airport who looked like she could use a friend.

It was time to fly home.

EPILOGUE

I have trouble sleeping on planes, trains, boats, buses, and cars. It's bed or nothing. Getting home required three flights: A five-hour flight to Doha, Qatar, a fifteen-hour flight to Dallas, Texas, then a nearly two-hour flight to Albuquerque, New Mexico. From there, I would have to drive an hour north to Santa Fe. My doctor gave me pills to help me sleep on the plane, but I figured I'd wait until the fifteen-hour flight to take one. Our flight left Nagpur, India at around 3:30 AM and would reach Doha, Qatar, around 8:30 AM.

I sat in my seat wide awake.

A flight attendant approached me. "Everyone on the plane is asleep but you. Are you alright?" she asked. "I'm fine," I replied. "I just can't sleep on planes". She crouched down in the aisle, and we had a quiet chat.

Her name is Bernadette, an attractive woman in her early to mid thirties. I learned that she is from one of the smaller countries in the Middle East and is a Flight Attendant Supervisor for Qatar Airways. She asked why we were in India, and I gave her the ten-minute version of how I came to have sons and daughters — and now families — in India.

She was intrigued. After asking some questions, she said that she would look for this book when it was published.

Bernadette reflected on how she was raised very conservatively and taught never to approach or initiate conversations with strangers. Working for an airline *requires* her to talk with strangers. Over the years she has learned that, when she engages with someone, each person's unique story opens up entirely new worlds for her.

As a result, she makes an effort to be 'open' to people and feels privileged to get a glimpse of someone else's world. She loves the feeling when her life intersects with a stranger's. The more this happens, the better she understands how deeply we are all connected.

Bernadette, I couldn't have said it better.

ACKNOWLEDGMENTS

I would like to thank my three awesome editors, Ed Rooney, Tracie O'Keefe, and Gloria Pendlay, for all their hard work. Writing is fun, but the editing process is tiresome. I reach the point when I know my words so well, I can look at mistakes and poor choices and fail to see them. My editors and friends make me look more talented than I am. No one knows as well as I do what a task it is to read and edit my ramblings over and over and over.

I have to thank my friend, Jane Rosemont, for the cover photography and design. Jane has won awards for her art, her photography, and her filmmaking. Having her agree to help out with this book cover was an honor.

I want to thank my wife, Judy, for lending her memory of details of our 2017 trip, when mine failed. It was also Judy's idea to put photos on my website, **www.rickcormier.com** , so that readers could see the places and people about whom I was writing.

Speaking of my website, it wouldn't exist without the talent and generosity of my *other* unofficially-adopted Indian son, Piyush Arora, who wished he could have accompanied us on this trip and shown us India's far north but was finishing his Masters degree at Purdue University. The others are jealous of Piyush. He flew to New Mexico in 2016 to spend Thanksgiving with us. He took a train here in 2017 and spent his Spring Break with us.

Lastly, I want to thank my test readers. Their job was tough: *"Read this and tell me what you liked and what you disliked — in a week."* My Indian test readers were also asked, "What did I get wrong?", while my non-Indian test readers were asked, "What didn't I explain well enough?" My test readers were Mike Cormier, Shubhi Jain, Rachna Jha, Mary Maverick, and Shivanshi Singh Rathaur.

ABOUT THE AUTHOR

During his years as a licensed psychotherapist, Rick Cormier conducted thousands of interviews. The first person he ever interviewed was India's Prime Minister Morarji Desai at the United Nations Plaza as research for a two-year undergraduate project on Mahatma Gandhi. Thus began his fascination with India and its culture.

When Rick was asked what prompted him to write "American Baapu", he said, "Whenever I tell people that we just returned from India where we stayed in five cities with five Indian families, people are fascinated to know how that came about. The story was getting too long to tell verbally. I was sure that 'MiXED NUTS' would be my last book . . . but maybe one more book was in order."

When he was 22, if you asked Rick what he wanted to be when he grew up, he would have answered, "a psychotherapist/cook/photographer/musician who writes books". Rick has managed to fit all of those activities into his life. Now that he has retired his license, he spends his time doing "Whatever is fun". That includes photography, writing books, drumming for several bands, teaching hand drumming in a public school, running community drum circles, and cooking for his wife.

After visiting the southwestern US in 2009 for their 25th wedding anniversary, Rick and Judy left their native New England in 2013 and moved to the suburbs of Santa Fe, New Mexico, USA. At 7000 feet altitude, snuggled within several mountain ranges, Rick, his wife, and his camera have never been happier.